SCOOTER NOMADS
BOOK ONE

SCOOTER NOMADS

BOOK ONE
OR
'WE DECIDED TO GIVE IT A GO'

BARDDRIEV PRESS

Copyright © Edsel F. Ward 2006

All rights reserved

First Edition
Paperback

ISBN: 978-0-9944992-9-5

Apart from any fair dealing for the purposes of
private study, research or review, as permitted
under the Copyright Act, no part of this book may
be reproduced by any process without permission.
Copyright of all text and photographs resides under
the Copyright, Designs and Patents Act with Edsel F. Ward.

Layout and Book Design: Brad Drew
Photographs and Maps: Edsel F. Ward
Cover Art and Design: Brad Drew

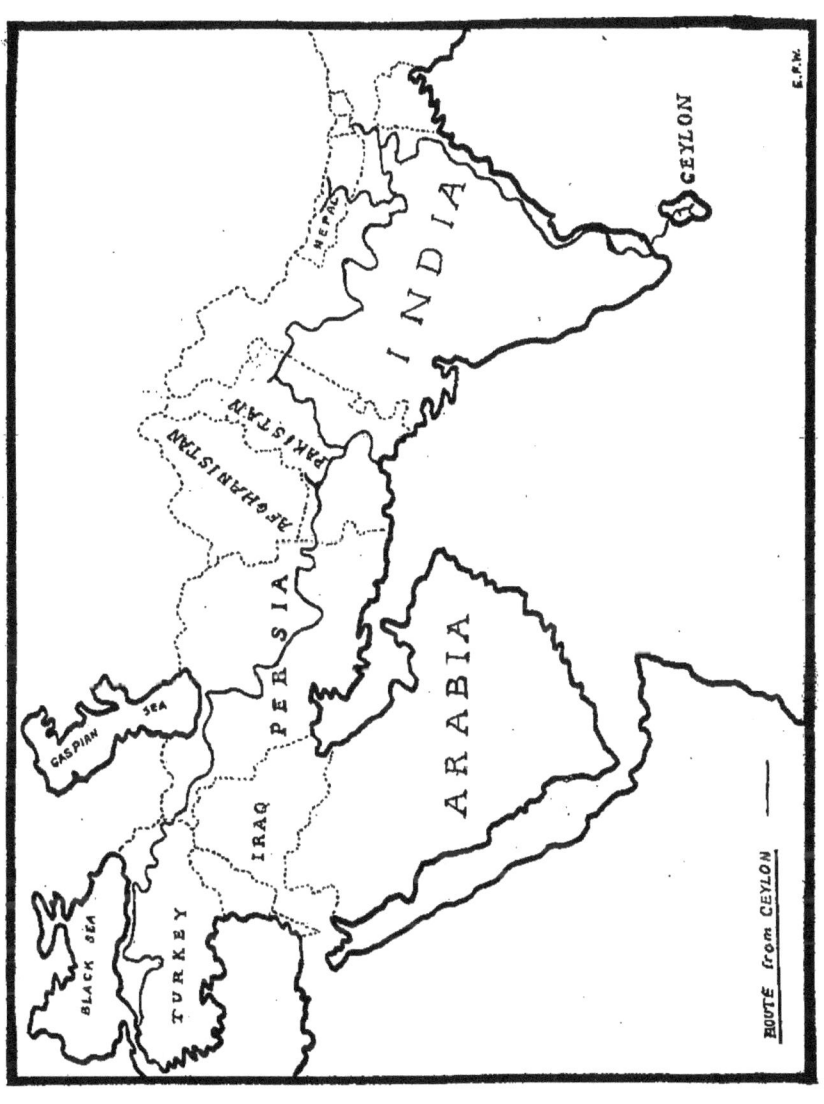

AUTHOR'S NOTE:

Photographs are later, black and white copies taken from original 1960, clear 35mm transparencies made during the course of the scooter adventure.

TABLE OF CONTENTS

Map 5

Author's Note 6

Table of Contents 7

Acknowledgements 8

Preface 9

Second Preface 11

Chapter One 13

Chapter Two 45

Chapter Three 69

Chapter Four 89

Chapter Five 131

Chapter Six 161

Chapter Seven 189

Chapter Eight 223

Chapter Nine 247

Chapter Ten 277

ACKNOWLEDGEMENTS

This manuscript covers the first half of a journey made by two young men in the 1960s: myself and Keith Basset. I wish to acknowledge the varied and much-valued assistance of those who helped me put this volume together.

First, to my wife, Lorraine, who tirelessly helped me with my grammar and corrected my spelling mistakes – a big job. Thank you also, to the other people who kindly proof-read this manuscript, picking up errors which we gratefully corrected.

Thank you, Ewan for the original transcription of this book. It is good to have such skills available in the family.

Finally, a sincere thank-you to Keith, for his comradeship on a journey lasting 12 months and covering two continents. Keith deserves a medal for staring at the back of my head for 24,000 miles, even if I was wearing a helmet for most of it. Keith rode pillion for eight weeks, with his arm in plaster, over rough and sometimes, unfriendly, terrain – it requires a special kind of person to do that.

It is my sincere hope that, when finished, this book will do justice to those who have helped me along the way.

EDSEL WARD

Flaxton, Queensland
February, 2006

PREFACE

To those who like to know the practical details and to any who are contemplating a similar journey ... ...

It had been a longstanding ambition of mine to do the overland journey from Ceylon to Turkey, then across Europe, but off the beaten track, if possible.

Keith Basset, my companion, was making plans for a trip to Canada when I discussed the idea with him. Keith and I knew each other well from our experiences as members of the Brisbane Bush Walkers Club and knew we could get along together under trying conditions. We decided to have a go.

Whatever vehicle we chose to use on the journey, we knew that we would probably have to manhandle it on occasions and it would also have to be rugged and economical. Our final choice was a Japanese fluid drive "Rabbit" Motor Scooter with a 200cc engine and a carrying capacity of 300 lbs this was nearly doubled on the trip. Our Scooter was christened "Mirrabooka", an aboriginal word for 'Southern Cross' and later became affectionately known as "Mirra".

I would like to thank those who helped us prepare the machine for the task which lay ahead of it. Sear and Gunn Pty Ltd. of Brisbane, for the special panniers they built to carry the equipment and which later on helped to save our lives on more than one occasion. Also R.& E. Steeden, Football Manufacturers, for body belts and other items including the special canvas water bags, without which we may have perished.

EDSEL WARD

Wynnum, Brisbane.
April, 1963

SECOND PREFACE

The original manuscript of "Scooter Nomads" was written, or rather completed, in 1963.

The sole remaining copy made a prolonged journey from Wynnum to Morningside and later Hawthorne, in Brisbane; to Flaxton and to Buderim, in the hinterland of Queensland's Sunshine Coast; to Canberra in the ACT; and then back to Flaxton.

This version of the manuscript, "restored to life" using the wonders of modern technology, was produced between October and December 2000. Having been asked by my father if I could save it from extinction should the last copy be lost, I decided to present a new version of the manuscript to my father for Christmas this year.

This will be my father's 71st Christmas; some thirty-seven years after the original manuscript was finished; and a few years more yet since the trip itself was made.

I have tried to keep the text as faithful to the original as possible. On the odd occasion that I could not resist an editor's touch, I made only minor changes to the wording that do not in any way change the story within.

My father once suggested that the manuscript, if reproduced in a format usable on a computer, could be "spiced" up and reworked into a novel that the publishers who once rejected it would accept. While this idea has merit, it seems to me an unwarranted corruption of what is already a wonderful tale – even if it is all true.

To my father then, whom I love very much, and to whom, with my mother, I will always be indebted, I give the new version of "Scooter Nomads". I hope that everyone who ever reads it will take away the message within its pages – one of the most special of all my father's qualities. In his words,

"We decided to give it a go."

EWAN F. WARD

Canberra, ACT.
December, 2000

CHAPTER ONE

I rolled as I hit the greasy road. Staggering to my feet, I shook myself to make sure I was all in one piece and then looked round to see how Keith had fared. He was just getting to his feet and was holding his wrist, trying to ease the pain of a fracture. As pillion passenger he had not been able to make a free escape from the skidding scooter and had taken the full impact on his left arm.

The scooter lay on its side just off the road in a deep gutter of greasy loam. Gear was strewn about and there was a strong smell of petrol in the air. I helped Keith to the roadside and sat him on a log just as dozens of wildly excited, dark brown locals, clad in loin cloths came running out of the jungle. I went to get the First Aid Kit from the bedding-roll still tied onto the tail rack but as I unrolled the bundle I was snowed under by the curious locals, who commenced picking up things to examine them. My hands were now full, for whenever I turned my back the natives would take full advantage and dive amongst the gear, souveniring, thus forcing me to stay close to the scooter.

Things were at their worst when a car pulled up and a Sinhalese dressed in whites jumped out.

"Can I help? I am a hospital attendant."

"You most certainly can," I said and handed him the First Aid Kit. Then, borrowing a large cane knife from a staring local, I got busy cutting bamboo splints for my helper and quickly returned to rescue the scooter from the marauders. I repacked and walked on the toes of the light-fingered locals, using my big boots to their full advantage.

When everything was lashed down I went to see the patient. He was looking a little happier as the Hospital Attendant finished off a neat job on his arm by putting on a sling.

"I will take your friend to the hospital if you like. It is fourteen miles away."

I agreed and thanked him.

The car was an old model Plymouth with six passengers jammed inside but it did not remain that way for long for the Attendant opened the door and forcibly dragged one of the passengers from the back seat to make room for Keith. The passenger resisted violently but he lost the battle and Keith was put inside and the door slammed shut.

I was still inquiring about the location of the hospital when the car was slipped into gear and roared off round the bend to be swallowed up by the green jungle, leaving me standing by the roadside together with the wide-eyed watchers.

I pushed my way back to the scooter. There seemed to be little damage to the machine as the specially made steel panniers on the sides had saved the day when we hit the patch of diesel oil covered by a layer of wet ox dung. We had only been three days in Ceylon and this was our first day on the road with our "Rabbit" scooter.

I heaved the scooter onto its wheels, started the motor, and bulldogged it back onto the bitumen through the sticky loam. With the help of two of the more intelligent bystanders, I made it and roared off in the wake of the Plymouth.

The thick vegetation was still dripping with moisture from the earlier downpour. As the road was still slippery, I rode with care. I had only travelled about eight miles when I came upon a car off the road and surrounded by a crowd of people, plus an elephant. I stopped to look.

Apparently the car had suffered a similar mishap to ours and had veered off the road into a deep gutter where it was now well and truly bogged in the thick red mud. The occupants of the car were Sinhalese and had borrowed one of the elephants working on timber nearby to pull the car out. The animal had been left with the problem and was moving around the car, gently feeling for a grip. Finally he wrapped his trunk under the back of the car and without any apparent effort lifted it and dragged it back on to the road.

Having seen the performance I mounted the scooter and rode off, pondering how handy an elephant might be. Rounding the next bend I nearly froze as I was confronted with the rear ends of two huge mounds of flesh, lumbering along side by side, carrying logs gripped between their tusks and trunk. I was doing about thirty miles per hour on the still wet road and a sudden braking would mean another skid and a possible collision with the animals. The only alternative was to drive between them. I crouched low over the handlebars to keep under the logs and slipped through between the rolling monsters. I gave a sigh of relief as I burst into the open and continued cautiously on.

I cruised past villages, coconut groves and paddy fields and it was almost dark when I stopped to inquire the whereabouts of the hospital. Luckily I had picked a doctor's residence and he gave me directions to the hospital, which I reached after dark. I parked at the entrance and with my helmet in my hand entered, and was met by a police sergeant.

"You will find your friend at the casualty ward on the first floor," he said. "Have you reported the accident to the police at Kahawatta?"

"No, but I will do it first thing in the morning," I promised him, "but now I want to find my friend."

*****

I walked up a long flight of steps to a corridor where I came to a queue of people, on the end of which was Keith, his arm still in the sling. There were about a dozen casualties before him and relatives were scattered along the length of the corridor, lounging on grass mats and blocking the passageway. As there was little I could do until Keith's arm was set, I returned to the policeman. After inquiring the whereabouts of the Government Rest House, I set off into the pitch-dark night and the outskirts of Ratnapura. ... ...

After an early breakfast at the Rest House next morning I rode to the Hospital where I found Keith propped up in bed in a ward full of other accident victims. He had not yet had any treatment but was due to have x-rays taken, along with other motor cycle victims. I did my best to cheer him up then left to report the accident to the police at Kahawatta.

I had driven as far as the Ratnapura garage when the motor started to play up. Inspection disclosed that the Heli-Coil in the cylinder head had worked loose and the motor was losing compression. Not feeling in the mood for maintenance I decided to leave the scooter at the garage and catch a bus to Kahawatta. On finding I had two hours to wait, I set out to explore the town.

Ratnapura is set deep in a valley between high mountains

with Adams Peak, 7,360 feet, dominating the northern side. This mountain is known locally as the 'Holiest Mountain in the World' and is sacred to the adherents of the Buddhist, Hindu, Muslim and Indian Christian religions.

The town itself is the centre of the gem industry in Ceylon. The name 'Ratnapura' means 'City of Gems'; gems have been worked in this area for the past 2,500 years, yielding sapphires, moonstones, rubies and cat's eyes. I paid my small admission fee and spent the two hours inspecting the collection in their gem museum. I had to make a bolt for the bus.

When at last the bus pulled up at the centre of a small village and the driver turned round and coughed out "Kahawatta", I jumped down to the road and looked up and down the street to make sure that there was no wild traffic coming, before crossing the road and heading for a signpost which said "Police".

Groups of people were lounging about in the shade of the palm leaf awnings of the bamboo shops and the only sign of activity was some ox-carts that were creaking their way down the road, their drivers sound asleep on the top of their loads. I followed the narrow track through the jungle and past the residential area with its grass and bamboo huts scattered amongst tall, slender coconut palms. The scantily clad locals were busy with their chores and only a few took time off to stare at me as I passed.

The police station, on the crest of a hill, had a commanding view of the village below and was built of stone with a six feet high wall round the perimeter, making it a small fort.

Going into the office I told my story to the sergeant. In broken English he told me I would have to wait until one of the English-speaking officers returned to make the report. I was invited to have tea while I was waiting and spent the next three hours conversing in sign language about the Great Dividing Range which cuts Australia in half, snakes, elephants, drivers licenses, and cricket. We had one interruption when two thieves were brought in and interrogated by two of the tougher constables who literally hammered confessions out of them and then marched them off to the cells at the rear of the building.

Eventually my man turned up and after hearing my account of the accident, dragged out a pile of forms which we filled in. By the time he had finished, the report looked like a chapter from "Gone with the Wind". The sergeant insisted I have an escort back to the village and in the company of a constable I entered the pitch-black night. Halfway down the track a long slender snake shot across our path in the beam of the torch and made us both freeze for a second. Native drums were beating in the village and for a moment or two I felt completely isolated in the black jungle.

On reaching the main road my escort departed, leaving me to wait for the last bus in the hurricane lamp lit street, which was deserted except for a few people squatting under a nearby awning. Five quiet minutes passed, then one by one people started appearing along the length of the street, gradually creeping forward to form a circle about me. They were all short in stature and I felt a little like Gulliver in Lilliput as they stared at me with large brown eyes. I spoke to them but they backed off, yabbering softly to each other. Suddenly a small boy raced off towards a hut and quickly returned with a tottery old man dressed in whites. A passageway was cleared for him as he approached and greeted me in English.

"Good evening Sir."

When I recovered from my surprise, I set about making friends with him. He acted as interpreter, explaining everything.

Suddenly an argument broke out among the group and much shouting and gesticulating took place with the victim a small boy who was hustled off in the direction of a shop. He returned smartly with a coconut in each hand and presented them to me.

The tops were lopped off and wishing the crowd health, I downed the coconut milk, dribbling it across my chin, much to the amusement of everyone. Next a bunch of bananas was thrust into my hand. I ate a few of them before another coconut was passed to me.

At this juncture the bus arrived, but I was not allowed to pay my own fare so in appreciation I made a speech from the bus step, which the old man translated. I waved goodbye to my friends, deeply touched by their genuine friendliness which, coming as it did from people unused to strangers, made a deep impression on me. This was but the first of many such experiences we were to have.

I spent that night on the floor of the Rest House as all the beds were occupied.

Next morning Keith was sitting up in bed with his arm set in plaster from the hand almost to the shoulder. He had told the doctor that he would be travelling on the back of a motor scooter and he wanted a solid job and the doctor had obliged. He was declared fit, so, armed with an x-ray and a statement from the doctor about the fracture, we returned to a waiting taxi. Keith was glad to be out in the fresh air again. His hospitalisation had been on the Free List and he had been pleased to be treated by Australian-trained doctors. The rest of the day was spent quietly at the Rest House, writing and taking stock of the situation.

Under the circumstances there was only one thing to do, go back to Colombo and see if we could get the scooter fixed. After seeing Keith off on the Colombo bus I loaded up and set out.

Eleven miles further on the scooter started to play up again and I pulled in under the overhanging roof of a would-be garage to try to fix it. The Heli-Coil had again worked loose but this time it was a workshop job. I was stuck! Not having any desire to remain there indefinitely, I asked the garage owner in sign language if he would get the scooter and me a lift to Colombo on a truck. He said he would help so I settled down for a long wait.

But I had not been settled long when several curious natives came to gaze at me and the mechanised rickshaw. They proceeded to poke and finger the scooter and me. My crash helmet particularly fascinated them. After much studying they finally accepted me and I was offered some betel nut to chew. Not wishing to offend I accepted and took the lime smeared leaf and nut and popped it into my mouth and started chewing. This amused my audience no end and they giggled and yabbered to each other as I slowly and reluctantly chewed the concoction. Some of them then came forward to demonstrate how the nut should be chewed, and the correct method of spitting out the red juice. This gradually developed into a long distance spitting competition, the target being a Pepsi Cola sign. At the first opportunity I got rid of the foul stuff, removing it quietly so that no one would be offended.

At this point a pith-helmeted rubber planter walked in,

"One of my boys told me you had broken down, can I be of any assistance?" he asked.

I had just finished explaining the situation to him when a Morris panel van pulled up for petrol. In no time my helmeted friend had secured a lift for the scooter and me in the van to Colombo. A space was cleared for the scooter amongst a number of apple cases in the back, leaving just enough room to squeeze in our gear and one of the passengers from the front, to give me a seat.

We moved off with the van riding heavily on the road and the driver trying his best to impress me with his driving as he darted in and out of traffic, narrowly missing heavily laden ox-carts and wandering people. Halfway to Colombo we stopped to take a drink of coconut milk and while I was drinking I heard a lot of conversation between the driver and the man in the back of the van. By the look on their faces they were talking about me. Feeling suspicious of the company, I finished my journey to Colombo where they drove me to our scooter agent, Colombo Trader, and unloaded the gear and scooter.

I offered them a few rupees for their trouble but was surprised when they refused payment. It was not until the following morning that I discovered the reason for this, they had taken a camera out of my rucksack, along with two films. When I discovered the theft I felt very annoyed with myself for being so foolish to leave a camera so handy to probing fingers. Luckily I had it insured, and I had learnt a valuable lesson.

Colombo Traders informed me that Keith was waiting in a hotel and I was packed off in a company car with our gear, leaving our sick scooter in the hands of the mechanic. Keith met me outside the dilapidated, red brick building and between us we got our gear up the long flight of rickety wooden steps to a room on the third floor. By Colombo standards the room was fair but the manager warned us to lock up before we left. Keith had located the YMCA and found it had a restaurant, so we locked our room and walked across a part of the city which was new to us, a district of tall buildings, narrow alleyways and clip joints. The dining room was a welcome sight and we made the most of our first meal since breakfast. On leaving the dining roam, we had to force our way past a pack of beggars who had congregated outside, in wait for victims as they left. If they got no results by direct begging they resorted to pick pocketing and pocket slashing with small razor edged knives which were freely used when possible. We ran the gauntlet for two blocks and returned to the hotel.

Next morning we ate breakfast in the company of six Chinese gentlemen, then went to report the theft of the camera to the police. They gave me no hope of getting the camera or films back and suggested I collect the insurance instead. Next stop was the garage where we met a concerned mechanic.

"I do not know how long your cylinder head will last; I suggest you try and get a new one if you intend carrying on," he said. A new cylinder head was out of the question for the present, but it was now we had to decide what we were going to do. We had a machine that was barely capable of pulling your hat off your head, a pillion passenger with his arm in plaster from finger to shoulder, and one driver to handle the sick, overloaded scooter across thousands of miles of unknown roads and conditions. Neither of us felt like turning back as we had barely begun the journey that we had been planning for the past eight months. I looked at Keith and said,

"Supposing we get the scooter fixed, I don't mind driving all the way, but will you mind bouncing on the pillion seat for 25,000 miles if your arm is not strong enough to drive?"

Keith thought for a while,

"Aw yes, suits me. We'll give it a go."

The following morning we finalised matters with the police and the insurance office and then went to see if our scooter was ready for the road. The mechanic, showing us the machine, shook his head and said,

"I have done all I can under the circumstances, but I doubt if it'll take you halfway across India. In fact I think you're crazy, attempting such a journey on a mechanically unsound machine."

I spent the remainder of the afternoon in a nearby bazaar bargaining for a few extras, which we needed for the trip.

On our way back to the hotel after dinner that evening, we were confronted by a tough looking youth who wanted to change money for us. We tried to discourage him but he would not take no for an answer and followed us to the hotel door. Keith made a quick retreat to our room but I decided to bargain with the money changer as I was about due to cash a cheque.

"How much per pound Sterling will you give me?"

"Fifteen," he said, holding up his fingers to make sure I understood.

"Ah! Run away, I know where I can get twenty."

He stood there with his mouth open for a moment, rocked by my statement, then, when he recovered, declared he would get me twenty and not to leave until he returned.

Ten minutes later he slipped quietly up the steps beside me and whispered confidentially,

"I get you eighteen?"

"No deal. Twenty or nothing," I said, even though I was tempted to take the eighteen.

I waved a five-pound Traveller's Cheque under his nose and

without a word he darted off again. He returned shortly with a pained expression on his face as though he had just stubbed his toe.

"I can get you, twenty," he said in sorrowful tones.

I tore the cheque out and started to fill it in. He almost threw a fit as he waved his arms.

"No-one can do this but the money changer," he cried. At the same time he snapped the cheque out of my fingers, ran down the steps, and turned into a narrow alleyway with me right on his heels, wondering if I had seen the last of my cheque.

He stopped in front of a small doorway and breathing heavily said,

"Come no further. It is forbidden. Here is money changer. Trust me."

I agreed, but was feeling that I had seen the last of my fiver when he suddenly returned with a fistful of rupees and counted them out to me. I checked them. Yes, I had my twenty all right, so now all I hoped was that they were not counterfeit.

I returned to the hotel and asked Keith if he would like to come for a stroll round the bazaar while I spent some of my hot money on film. We cut straight into the bazaar where we were confronted by everything from vagrants to dope pedlars. Eventually, we came to a cluster of shops selling photographic equipment, and after surveying the layout, picked on one that appeared to have the best range of films and entered.

Hardly had I crossed the threshold when I was enveloped in a wave of yabbering salesmen who wanted to 'sell me good camera'. I pushed my way through to the counter ignoring them all until I found one who looked like the manager. I was about to ask him the price of film when he got in first,

"How much for your camera?" he asked. "What price?"

Helped by his assistants he argued, screamed and made me offers, in an effort to lever the camera away from me. Bedlam ensued. I hugged my camera, half expecting someone to cut the strap as they crowded around me. However, they gradually simmered down when they realised they were wasting their breath and that I really came to buy film. A haggle over prices now ensued. After ten minutes I found myself in possession of two colour films at better than the right price. I examined them, paid up, then rejoined Keith and continued our stroll back to the hotel, feeling happy with the evening's transactions.

To cut down on weight we donated our Li-los to the Colombo Boy Scouts next morning, then got down to the business of loading up the scooter in preparation for the road before a critical audience. By the time we were ready to leave, it seemed as though half of Colombo had come to see us off. It felt good to be mobile again.

Outside Kandy we paused to admire the Royal Botanical Gardens which date back to 1371 and are reputed to be the most beautiful in the East. They take in an area of some 150 acres and have species of tropical plants and trees from all over the world. Time went too quickly and we were again on the move, climbing up the last grade into the cool of Kandy.

Entering the city, we passed Buddhist monks walking along the streets with their saffron robes making a splash of colour against the greenery.

We cruised round the city until we found a parking spot under a shady tree by the Temple of the Tooth. We joined a host of pilgrims in a visit to the Temple – but instead of paying homage to Buddha, we admired the structure and the ornate woodcarvings. Leaving the Temple was the hardest part. We were pestered by beggars and souvenir sellers who, unfortunately for them, mistook us for American tourists, who were prevalent in the area, and it was not until we were able to ride off on the scooter that we escaped them.

As we neared the hostel on the outskirts of the town I had to dodge a long parade of elephants heading for the river. They had been working on the timber nearby and now it was time for their daily bath. We stood on the riverbank and watched as they entered the water with great gusto, splashing, trumpeting, blowing bubbles, and in general causing a tidal wave. The elephants were joined by working buffaloes, which preferred to walk quietly into the water and stand with their heads exposed, in a "could-not-care-less" attitude.

When the elephants had worn cuff their excess energy they lay down in the shallow water and waited for their mahouts to scrub them down. The wiry mahouts got busy on their own animals with large scrubbing brushes and scrapers, giving the animals a thorough clean-up, and making sure that all the vermin were off after the day's work in the jungle. The mahouts amused us as they examined the huge ears, eyes and almost crawled into the elephants' mouths to make sure the beasts were clean. The elephants seemed to enjoy their bath and when they were finally taken out the water their mahouts tried to earn themselves a quick rupee from the audience by selling rides on their animals.

We spent the evening studying a map, working out a round trip in the tea country for the following day.

It was just after dawn and the air was cool and crisp as we drove through a stirring Kandy and took the ox-cart cluttered road to Gampola. Buffaloes plopped their way through the muddy paddy fields while elephants worked on timber in the lush jungle, disturbing colonies of monkeys. Thousands of colourful birds rose screaming from the treetops, almost out-doing the din of the monkeys.

By the time we had reached the five thousand feet mark, tea plantations had become a familiar sight and we were contouring across carpeted slopes only broken now and then by stands of cinchona trees towering about the tea plants. For a backdrop there were the rugged, jungle-clad eight thousand feet peaks dominating the skyline and deep gorges with spectacular waterfalls thundering into the depths. On the higher slopes tea pickers were busy filling their baskets for the great white tea factories perched on the crest of the hills above the plantation.

At Nuware-Eliya we asked if it was possible to visit a tea factory. It was suggested we try a factory outside the town.

The factory turned out to be the usual four story, corrugated iron building with "Edinburgh Tea Factory 1934" inscribed over the entrance. We passed through big double doors and into the modern office where we were met by the foreman who regretted that the factory was not working as the pickers had finished on this particular plantation. But in their absence, he added, we would be able to have an uninterrupted tour.

We were led up a long flight of wooden stairs to the top floor where the manufacture of the tea starts. Here was a huge drying room, where the leaves were brought up on a conveyor belt after grading and then put onto big trays in racks where air at 190°F flowed over them. We worked our way downwards past drying rooms, chopping machines and blowers and on to the ground floor again where we were shown the machinery that makes the place tick. If nothing else, I learnt that it takes 2300 shoots to make one pound of tea.

We thanked the guide for our tour and asked him for some samples but he politely refused and instead asked us to sign the Visitor's Book.

Next morning we set our course northward for Sigiriya or the fortress in the Sky. After travelling across the flat, dry, scrubby country, we were glad to pull into the Rest House about three quarters of a mile from the Sigiriya. There we took a long drink, swapped our crash helmets for slouch hats, parked the scooter under a shady tree and then set off to explore "The Fortress in the Sky".

Sigiriya means Lion Rock and it was not until we had found our way to the entrance to the four hundred feet high rock that we realised the significance of the term. The approach was guarded by two huge stone-carved lion's paws, all that is left of an enormous brick and plaster lion which towered above the ground and guarded the entrance to the fortress.

The Fortress, together with its palace, was built by King

Kasyapa I after he killed his father, King Dhatur Sena, in 477 A.D. Kasyapa ruled for eighteen years before his brother, who had been driven into exile and had raised an army in India, returned to challenge him to a battle on the open plains in which Kasyapa was defeated. The brother then returned to the old capital, Anuradhapura, leaving the Fortress to decay over the centuries.

We passed between the lion's paws and started to climb up a staircase of two thousand steps, many of them now steel for the originals were badly eroded and no longer safe. The tourist industry has crept into the area and we had to pay an admission fee before going to the top. Past the initial climb we followed walled passages decorated with frescoes some 1500 years old depicting processions of Buddhist pilgrims and native women. We were joined by a party of Buddhist pilgrims who delighted in showing us round and when we had reached the summit they took us on a Cook's tour of the Palace remains, the brick fortifications and a number of slime covered wells that were once the water supply for the Fortress. We were amazed at the size of the place and the rather well preserved condition of the ruins, for, from the bottom, one would never dream that such a place ever existed on top of the great rock. We wandered around for hours, then made the steep descent down the old staircase, past the lion's paws and ancient fighting towers, to the path which led back to the rest house.

Keith (on left), 'Mirrabooka' and the Author.

'The approach was guarded by two huge stone-carved lion's paws ...'

View from the Summit of 'Sigiriya'

After a short breather, we mounted up and set off to Dambulla, a place that is noted for its rock temples – one of which houses a 47 feet recumbent Buddha carved from solid rock. We arrived in Anaradhapura, the ancient capital of Ceylon, to discover that a new town was being built outside the boundaries of the ruined city.

The following day we explored this first capital of the Sinhalese Kings, which dates back more than three thousand years. We visited the Bo tree, which grew from a branch of the original tree under which Buddha sat waiting for enlightenment 2,500 years ago. It was fascinating to think that Anaradhapura in its prime had a population of over three million, making it one of the largest ruined cities we were to see on our trip. Of all the city's sights I think the most spectacular was the enormous dome-shaped Ruwanvili Dogoba built by one of Ceylon's warrior kings. Around the base of this huge Dogoba is carved a life size relief of stone elephants which are perfect in every way, even to the carved chains around their feet. While visiting the Dogoba we were accompanied by a monk and given garlands of flowers to wear as well as a handful of crushed flowers for an offering to Buddha.

We visited three of the Dogobas and the remains of the reputed nine storied, one thousand roomed palace – now only marked by a thousand stone monoliths, leaning at odd angles and surrounded by untold numbers of stone beams and bricks. No matter where we walked we could see huge slabs of cut stone lying about the ground, some of them standing out like giant tooth picks under the shade of the big trees that have been planted to keep this ruined city a sanctuary. The complete area is sacred and is watched over by monks who live in some of the smaller monasteries.

Our next job was to buy provisions for our trip into Wilpatu National Park, as we were not sure if food was available there. The map read twenty miles to the Park turnoff so after shaking off some troublesome locals, we set out along the flat bitumen road.

Opposite a ramshackle shop was a sign post which read "Wilpatu National Park 14 Miles". The road we must follow was obviously designed to discourage poachers for it was as rough and rugged as they come.

First we passed through a village where we were chased by pigs and in the process almost collected a few wandering cows. The country was flat, dry and scrubby, and as we progressed the road got worse. We were driving in great washed out wheel tracks that were bedded with sand and more than once we were hard put to remain upright. As this was the first really rough road on which I had driven the loaded scooter, I had to develop a new technique and learn to drive all over again. The rucksacks took a bashing as they whacked against trees and sods of dry earth and just for variety we would occasionally do the Skaters Waltz in soft sloppy mud until we sank to a stop. It was a drive to be remembered.

We eventually came to a stockade-like fence with two big wooden gates blocking the road, where we were challenged by a warden in uniform.

"Permit," he asked holding out his hand.

Now this was one thing I had forgotten about, but we had not come completely unprepared – for I had a letter of introduction from the Queensland Forestry Department and the National Parks Association of Queensland, as well as a letter from the Lord Mayor of Brisbane, complete with a huge official red seal. I dug them out and handed them to the Ranger, who read through each letter. When he got to the red seal his expression changed and he lost no time welcoming us to the park and opening the gates for us.

"You may go," he said, "but make sure you take no longer than half an hour because it is close to the time when animals come out. You must drive quietly so as not to frighten them. Look out for leopard, boar and, elephant. Good luck."

We thanked him, then rode off over the improved track

through the five mile Intermediate Zone to a second check point, where we again had to show the letters before being allowed to pass.

We were now in the Park proper and driving along a hard-baked, dusty track through thick, wild scrub plaited with wicked looking thorn bushes. For the first time I realised how awfully exposed we were sitting on the scooter and I felt easy meat for a hungry cat. On the way I saw several animals moving in the scrub and even though I was curious, found myself twisting the throttle a little harder.

We broke into a clearing in the centre of which was the Park Administration Centre, surrounded by a barb wire fence. Pulling up in front of the neatest bungalow, I asked a boy where the Chief Ranger could be found. I had barely asked the question when the gentleman I was seeking appeared and introduced himself as Percy De Alies, Chief Warden, and asked for my credentials, which he studied carefully for some five minutes before handing them back.

"This is highly irregular to enter Wilpatu without a permit but as you are a fellow Ranger I would like both of you to be my guests. I suggest you get the scooter under cover before the monkeys run off with it."

In his office, we met Ricardo Moragas, a young Spanish

lawyer on his way home from three years study in the U.S.A. Keith took up conversation with Ricardo while I tackled the Chief Warden, firing a barrage of questions about the park at Percy, as he preferred to be called. When he realised we were genuinely interested in Wilpatu he offered to take us for a ride in the jeep and show us the real park, in the evening when all the animals would be out. Percy, Ricardo, Keith, a boy with a rifle and myself climbed into the jeep which was parked outside and rode out of the compound. Percy knew all the tracks and short cuts blindfold and as we bounced our way over the terrain, he pointed out Red Deer, wild boar and different species of monkeys.

He proudly told us that Wilpatu National Park is the largest park in Ceylon, covering an area of 136,000 acres and bounded by a broad Intermediate Zone, which acts as a Park buffer. There were twenty-six lakes in the park, most of which were fresh water and the highest point was a 312 feet high hill. Most of the Park was dense forest and scrub which broke into open gilla country (stunted scrub) round the lakes. We pulled up by one of the lakes and tried to sneak up on flocks of cranes, cormorants and storks but the noise of the motor frightened them and they rose as a cloud which almost blotted out the sky.

We moved on, heading into thick scrub, when suddenly Percy

jerked to a halt.

"Ssh!"

We sat breathless, peering around to see what had caused the sudden excitement. I noticed a peculiar smell in the air, then suddenly about twenty yards in front of us there emerged from the thick vine-tangled scrub an enormous leopard. I could hardly believe my eyes for here, quite close, was a true wild leopard which made zoo specimens look like kittens.

We barely breathed as we watched the powerhouse of muscle stalk across the track and disappear into the scrub. No-one spoke and the only sound in the still air was an occasional high pitched, blood-curdling scream somewhere up in front of us. Without a word Percy let the jeep silently roll down the incline for about a hundred yards and then stopped.

Across to our left in the centre of a clearing was a herd of Spotted Deer, about twenty in number, feeding quite happily and apparently unaware of the impending danger. As if by command all the deer suddenly froze, sniffing the air with their heads held high. For two or three minutes nothing happened, then the does and fawns milled around in a close, nervous bunch while the straight horned bucks circled around the perimeter, calling to each other in the same high pitched squeal, we had heard earlier. They obviously knew there was something after them. One beautifully marked spotted specimen cautiously moved towards a downwind thicket then stopped, rigid. Suddenly he gave an ear-piercing scream – in a body the herd turned and bolted, the big buck being last away. Almost at the same instant from out of the thicket came the leopard in a gigantic spring, which brought him just short of his dinner. He gave chase for a few yards, but, too late! He had done his dash! The herd crashed through the open scrub in full flight, leaving a panting, hungry leopard staring after them. Disappointed, the big cat slunk away into the scrub in search of an easier dinner.

The light was failing fast as Percy meandered the jeep back to the bungalows, dodging deer and an occasional wild buffalo. As we pulled up in front of the bungalow and I climbed out of the jeep I felt well satisfied with our glimpse of life in the jungle.

After dinner, while Keith and Ricardo were talking, I got into conversation with Percy who could not understand why there were not any elephants and leopards in our Australian forests. After a fish breakfast next morning with the whole family, I was allowed to photograph Percy's wife and daughter in their beautifully coloured silk saris, which they had donned, for the occasion. They then offered to feed two young sloth bears that were chained up to a tree near the house while I took another photo. The sloths were friendly little, long, black-haired fellows, with white noses and long curved sharp claws and pointed teeth, the signs of a formidable opponent if they got upset. These bears are a feature of Wilpatu.

Being in the mood for photographing animals I decided to have a go at the monkeys, which were there in thousands.

"You will never photograph those monkeys; but you can try," Percy grinned. "Look out for wild boar and snakes if you get too deep in the scrub."

"Thanks," I said, and moved out cautiously. I spotted a group of three monkeys playing yo-yos on the end of a long branch quite close to the ground. Creeping forward with my camera cocked and at the ready, I got within twelve feet of them and was about ready to press the shutter when hell broke loose. The previously quiet forest was filled with the noise of hundreds of screaming monkeys swinging from branch to branch and tree to tree, showering leaves on the tufted grass below. My three models had disappeared amongst the mad multitude.

"Yes," I thought, "Percy was right."

I made several more attempts, but instead of getting my photos, I found myself being lured deeper into the forest by the band of retreating monkeys.

After that performance, we loaded the scooter up and Percy escorted us over the rough road to the main highway. There we said goodbye to Percy. Ricardo was going to try to catch the next day's ferry to India from Mannar. As there were two days between ferrys we decided to try to keep Ricardo company and make the crossing with him, so we too set our course for the ferry port of Mannar.

Leaving Ceylon

CHAPTER TWO

Our introduction to India was a lively one!

Before we could get into the country, we had to pass through the customs barrier at the port of Dhanushkodi. This entailed a wait which, though long, was an entertaining one, for near us the police were searching the goods of an Indian Merchant, while his four wives and porters looked on. A Customs Officer directed operations from a cane chair with the aid of a long stick which he pointed at the bundles to be broken open. The police boys were busy ripping bundles and trunks open and throwing toys, silks, cottons, kitchen utensils and ironmongery on to the platform.

The last trunk, when broken open, revealed several layers of clothing – under which was a large quantity of bar soap. Eyeing it with suspicion, the Customs Officer ordered it to be broken open with bayonets and the merchant protested loudly, waving his arms about as he shouted at the police.

Suddenly the bayonet struck something solid and shiny. It was a gold watch!

This was about the end of the chapter for the merchant, for now the police boys, under orders, were tearing up everything they could get their hands on, to see what else he had tried to smuggle into the country. Four watches were found and the place turned into bedlam as the excited police took it out on the screaming merchant and his wives, who were obviously denying everything. The resisting man was dragged off to an office where he was thrust inside. The door was slammed, and his wives were left to continue the argument with the police outside.

Many of the peasants going through Customs had their rice and tea tipped out on to benches and sifted, and as a result they were losing a lot of their valuable food. On the other hand the Customs could not be blamed for doing this, as they had a tough job trying to keep smuggling down and they had to take every precaution. It was four hours from the time of our arrival before they got around to checking the scooter and then it was only after I had complained to the man in charge. The Carnet was filled out, the engine and chassis numbers checked, and the machine was thoroughly searched under the strict supervision of an officer before it was cleared.

At six thirty our train creaked out of Dhanushkodi, scooter aboard, and had hardly cleared the station when a brawl started in our overloaded carriage. A party of peasants in front of us had been trying to get a chap to move along the seat he was occupying and he, resisting, sparked off a free for all. One wrinkled old crone was using a brass water urn like a pile-driver on the head of a trespasser who had already gone down for the count.

Keith and I put on our cash helmets.

The brawl simmered down and all was quiet until the first stop, where a host of people was poised, ready to storm the train. As it screeched to a halt, the newcomers charged the carriage, climbing in through windows as well as the doors. Two windows and shutters in our carriage were smashed by the invading mob which, having broken through, threw in their pots and pans and bundles and came clambering in after them, fighting with those already in possession as they came.

Our shutter was left alone for several stations but was finally attacked. The Indian beside me was wide-eyed and frightened as the mob outside started bashing at the shutter to break it down. He barred his arms against it to try and stop them, at the same time exchanging some fiery conversation with them in Tamil. Just as the shutter was about ready to cave in, I slammed my big boots up on to the base of it and held it tight.

The invaders, unable to shift it, called off the attack and I could hear them talking it over before they made a final attempt to break in. This too failed and our Indian companion turned and gave us a betelnut grin as a group of happy souls started singing behind us. The singing kept up for half an hour before passengers objected and silenced them with the urns!

By nine o'clock we had reached the road head of Mandanam, where we disembarked. As the train moved off a head popped out of the carriage in front and Ricardo waved goodbye.

In our first big Indian City, Madurai, next day, we drove through crowded streets where near naked coolies were working like beasts of burden pushing great barrows loaded with grain. Pulling up outside the State Bank of India we were hailed to by an English speaking voice.

"Hey Aussie."

Somebody had recognised our AUS plate. A short spectacled man in whites greeted us and introduced himself as Ken - a missionary from New Zealand. Since he spoke Tamil he offered to accompany us into the overcrowded building and make sure we were understood.

While our Travellers Cheques were being cashed, I was amused by the boys who were acting as bank runners, for they were very dark skinned and wore colourful red and black turbans with contrasting white coat and trousers from under which black splayed feet protruded. Their sole purpose in life was to dart from desk to desk carrying papers and delivering cups of tea. Our business completed, we parked the scooter at the railway station while Ken took us on a tour of the city.

We drove along crowded, busy streets with Ken sitting on the horn all the way, for the people of Madurai appeared to be stone deaf and would not move out of the way. The car had to bump some of them before they would move.

Ken also warned us of the traffic hazards in South India, especially the buffaloes, which were particularly bad and most unpredictable. They had caused many major accidents and occasionally charged vehicles.

The truth of his words was proved that same afternoon for we did not see a motor vehicle for the rest of the day, only ox-carts, donkeys, buffaloes, goats and, of course, innumerable people wandering aimlessly all over the road.

Travel was very slow – we did not know what the animals would do and the people were just as bad. I drove for most of the day with my thumb pressed on the horn but this had no effect, as everybody, and everything, seemed to be stone deaf ......

The motor started coughing soon after leaving Tiruchchirappalli next morning. As it finally cut out, we rolled to a stop under a large shady tree. Inspection disclosed that the coil had burnt out, so, hitching a ride on a passing bus, I returned to the city.

I alighted at the terminus and the centre of Tiruchi's workshop where wheelwrights were busy manufacturing ox-carts. Further down the street, thin, wiry workers, clad in loincloths were working in deep saw-pits cutting the logs with primitive saws.

In the A.A. Office with the help of an English-speaking mechanic, I bought a new coil, but now another problem arose. The only 12 volt coil in Tiruchi was a heavy duty one made for trucks.

Somehow we had to fix it on to our machine. A special bracket would be needed to carry it. The owner of the Tiruchi motor cycle shop set about making one from a steel plate, using a cold chisel, hammer, and brute force – the only tools available. In spite of this he did a good job. The coil was attached and we were quickly on our way.

On one of the long, narrow wooden bridges just outside the town the scooter spluttered to a halt again. Dirty petrol this time! Cleaning out the dirt (which included everything from hair to moths) was a great risk for several times we were all but trampled into the ground by runaway oxen pulling overloaded wagons. However, we survived and mounted the scooter again, this time clearing Tiruchi on the third attempt.

Ten miles north of the city we ran into a new traffic hazard: peasants winnowing grain on the road. These people very seldom see a motor vehicle of any description on this good bitumen and naturally think the road is for their use and an excellent place to winnow grain.

For the next fifty miles we weaved in and out of piles of threshed grain, dodging people who would not move for anything. By the time we got to the end of these stretches we were most uncomfortable, with chaff itching down our shirts as well as fine dust in our eyes, in spite of our goggles. This was but a preview, for all the way up the east coast of India we were to get this from time to time. ....

At the village called Wandur we decided to eat before returning to the Dak Bungalow to sleep. The village street was lit with hurricane lamps and the cool night air vibrated with beating drums and chanting. We walked past grass and bamboo huts to a place which looked like an eating house.

Entering the low stone and mud building we passed through a narrow door and stepped into a long rectangular room which had big black teak beams supporting the ceiling, and earth for a floor. The air was thick with smoke from slush lamps and smelt strongly of burning fat and curry. Hungry, rice-eating customers squatted on grass mats gorging themselves from the low teak slab tables. We found ourselves two vacant mats, sat down and made eating signs to a boy who immediately went to get mine host. Two banana leaves and two large glasses of water were placed in front of us, and after an arm-waving session with the manager, a boy appeared from out of the smoke and dumped two huge dollops of rice on the leaves. This was followed by three small wooden bowls, which we inspected carefully. We discovered that number one bowl contained marble sized potatoes with brown gravy, number two bowl had pieces of goat meat with a medium curry, the third one contained a flaming hot curry complete with capsicums.

We peered around the room to see how the others were eating their food, then tipped bowls one and two into the rice, sprinkled on a dash of the curry, and began mixing the concoction with our hands. For the first time we had to eat rice entirely with our hands and for a start found it very hard, as the brown goo slipped between our fingers before it reached our mouths, dripping back on to the banana leaf again. This was no good, so we took a second look to study techniques, then had another try. This time more successful. However, every few mouthfuls I was forced to pour large quantities of water down my neck in order to subdue the curry fire burning inside me and making me sweat profusely.

Everything has its humour and this time it was Keith. He was having trouble finding his mouth with his left hand and instead was decorating his ginger beard with rice grains.

We had barely cleared our banana leaf, when the boy returned to dump more rice on the banana leaf. Eventually, we got him to understand that we had had enough, so he went to get black coffee for us instead.

We drank coffee from clay bowls and studied the other customers wolfing down enormous quantities of rice and wondered how much of this mixture the human body could take before it burst. With these thoughts in mind we paid our bill and left for the bungalow ....

We had barely covered eighty miles the next morning when the scooter played up again and coughed to a halt. The Helicoil in the cylinder head had come right out and now we were in a real fix. There was only one thing to do, try for a lift into Madras in the hope of getting it fixed. We had not long to wait before a truck pulled up and after a little bargaining we organised a ride into Madras for the scooter and ourselves.

The A.A. gave me little hope of getting our machine fixed and suggested we park it in their garage over night.

We considered the situation next morning over breakfast and discussed the possibility of getting one of the agents to fly a new cylinder head to us. Halfway into town a big American car pulled up beside us and English voice hailed us.

"Would you like a lift?"

The driver introduced himself as Mr. Collins, the manager of a tobacco company in Madras, who asked us what we were doing wandering around Madras. As we drove, our story gradually unfolded. He looked very thoughtful.

"Why not come to my office?" he suggested, "and see what we can work out."

The office was a big place, full of electric fans and servants dressed in whites. We settled ourselves in comfortable chairs and had tea served to us while we discussed the problem of the scooter. Suddenly, Mr. Collins had an inspiration and rang a friend of his, Mr. Standford, an engineer with the new Royal Enfield factory which was just being built outside the city. After an involved conversation Mr. Collins hung up and, stroking his handlebar moustache, said he thought his friend would be able to help us. He suggested we take the head to the factory as soon as we finished our tea. This we did, and there met Cdr. Stanford, an engineer brought out from England to organise the new factory.

We showed him the head, which he studied carefully for a few moments.

"I believe I can fix it for you. Leave it with me for a day or so then drop back and with a bit of luck we will have a new cylinder head."

Mr. Collins decided to show us Madras and took us on a sightseeing tour.

The city had probably never looked so clean before, as

preparations were nearing completion for the arrival of the Queen the following afternoon. Along the streets, work parties were busy painting roundabouts and road signs. They were slapping paint over themselves as well as the signs, and I doubt if any of them had ever used a paintbrush before. At three o'clock next afternoon we took up our position opposite Government House. As the minutes passed, the crowds grew thick along the route until people were jammed in ten and twelve deep. Colourfully dressed police with tall red and black turbans and long bamboo batons lined the barriers. The population of Madras seemed to have swelled by several millions, and I doubt if half of them knew what they had come to see.

A heavy police guard had been thrown around Government House, and just in case of trouble, the riot squad had been scattered around the perimeter of the main entrance.

We still had some time to wait so I decided to try and get some photos of the dashing policemen. I pushed my way through the crowd and walked across the open square to where the most glamorous man was standing. I expected to be stopped by the police but instead was allowed past with a salute when I gave them a friendly nod and a wink. Walking straight up to an immaculate sergeant dressed in black, red and white sitting on a beautiful black horse, I presented my camera.

Immediately he straightened up like a ramrod for the picture but was thrust aside by his superior officer who was also mounted.

The officer was a tall, dandified fellow, dripping with braid and looked most hurt at not being approached first for his picture. I now had to try to satisfy them both, so I manoeuvred into a position to get them both into the picture and pressed the shutter. They both grinned like satisfied cats, leered at each other, then rode off.

There was a ring of four rows of police outside the gate and just for the heck of it I thought I would see how far I could penetrate. I took two more photos of ordinary constables as I edged my way forward to the big gate where I was stopped by a major who asked to see my passport and papers. He spoke poor English and I was doing fine until another officer appeared on the scene and asked for my special pass. I pleaded ignorance and said, "What special pass?"

"You cannot enter without a special pass," was the reply. "I suggest you return to your place in the crowd."

Seeing that I was beaten, I thanked the officer very much and returned to Keith across the road.

Just before the Queen arrived, a mob that must have seen her further up the road came bursting down a side street in a wave that broke into the square. In an instant, the police and Gurkha reinforcements formed up in a line and waded into the mob with long cane batons, pushing them back the way they had come.

A stampede started – the mob was going in all directions.

Keith and I got behind a tree to avoid being trampled underfoot as the tidal wave swept our way. Half an hour later, when things were normal again, the Queen and Prince Philip put in an appearance.

It was now late and too dark for photos as they drove into Government House, but I doubt if I could have taken one anyway because of the jostling, screaming mob.

As soon as the Queen disappeared inside the gates the mob broke loose again, bursting through barriers and stopping all traffic. The police and riot squad again moved amongst the mob with their canes, breaking them up and trying to restore order. We moved in the lava flow of people and were carried into town.

Next day Mr. Collins stopped by to tell us that the job on the head was done and it had been successful, and that we could pick it up the following day. This was the best news for a long time and to celebrate we went shopping and brought provisions for our anticipated return to mobility.

Mr. Standford was very pleased with the job and said he felt confident that it would get us through, and also gave us a new spark plug to go with it. We could not thank him enough, for his help and we considered ourselves extremely lucky in finding probably the only place in India where we could have got the job done and done well, and what is more, for gratis.

We said goodbye to Mr. Collins, then reassembled the scooter. The job completed, I took the scooter for a run and was as pleased as Punch with our like-new machine.

It was two thirty by the time we had packed and the people with whom we had been staying gave us a pleasant surprise by presenting us with a rice pudding. The night before we had been telling them that in Australia we usually ate rice in the form of puddings and as a parting gesture the wife had made us this enormous pudding, which between us we managed to polish off.

After another goodbye, we made for the open road ... ...

*****

On our proposed route northward we had two alternatives. One was via the main trunk road to Bombay, Bangalore then via the high country and the trunk road to Indore, Jaipur, Agra and Dehli.

The other was straight up the east coast to Calcutta and then across, allowing us, if we wanted, to visit Darjeeling and Nepal without back tracking.

The first route was more or less the main road across India, passing through many interesting places, but to us there was something missing. We wanted to try and get off the beaten track if we could and meet the different types of people. At the same time, we would probably get a bit of extra adventure thrown in. The route up the east coast looked like the answer.

The A.A. office in Madras advised us that the route, although there was a bitumen road for part of the way up the coast, was inadvisable because of river crossings and trackless detours, particularly across the Ganges Delta. But if we took this route we would be able to visit Darjeeling and Nepal. We decided to have a go.

It was a cloudy afternoon as we cruised along the smooth bitumen road, dodging ox-carts with their huge loads, and side stepping people walking right in the middle of the road. We were doing about 30 mph when we cruised up behind one of those characters. I started to blow the horn about fifty yards away but he appeared not to hear so I slowed down, keeping the horn blasting all the time.

I was about thirty feet off this middle-aged peasant, clad in loincloth and turban, when he started to meander all over the road. As I drew abreast of him he swayed in our direction and almost under the wheel. I swerved violently, almost biting the bitumen as I threw the scooter over in an endeavour to miss him. I thought I had succeeded, but I had not allowed for the overhanging rucksack, which clouted his legs and the long, hooked stick he was carrying. The impact threw the stick and sent the jaywalker spinning across the road in a heap. As soon as I could I pulled up and we both ran back to see if any damage had been done. He was in the process of getting onto his feet when he saw us, and a complete change came over him. We could read it in his eyes.

"White men!"

In a flash he fell back on the ground again and put on an act that a film star would have envied. He rolled round holding various parts of his body as though he had been mortally wounded.

Keith and I looked at each other, spellbound for a second or two, for we knew we had not done any serious damage to him.

Just then a Land Rover pulled up and two Indians got out and came over to see what had happened. On being told our story they had a look at the writhing man, spoke to him, then turned and told us to give him a rupee and he would be cured. We felt a little annoyed at having been caught, for we should have known better, but I dug into my pocket and tossed him a few annas. Immediately the pain ceased.

Next evening, we found ourselves midway between two huge rivers, the Krishana and Godavari.

We decided to drive until we came to the Godavari and there make camp. But it was dark and we were still driving when the road suddenly became extremely rough. Thinking we must have been on the wrong road, I started to swing the scooter from side to side so the headlight might give us a clue as to our whereabouts. On the left the headlight shone on to water – on the right, nothing, so I pulled up to have a better look.

We were on a high, narrow bank running parallel with the river and falling away sheer on both sides. Across the water we could see lights of Rajahmundry shining, so we rode on into a village where our way was barred by a chain across the road. We pulled up beside a line of a dozen-or-so trucks parked on the roadside. Leaving Keith to guard the scooter I went to investigate. Set back off the road were some poorly lit Governmental buildings where I hoped I could get some information.

I walked through the open door into a dusty office overburdened with ancient office equipment; a heavy spectacled man was seated behind a desk, so I asked him exactly where I was.

"You are at the head of the Godavari delta, at a place called Konvur," he said. "If you wish to cross with the truck convoys tomorrow morning, you will have to get a permit. I might warn you that the drive across the four weirs is dangerous and it's entirely at your own risk."

"Anything else?" I enquired.

"Yes. The convoy leaves at eight o'clock and it will cost you two rupees."

"Is there anywhere we can camp for the night, maybe in the grounds?"

"No! You'll be killed and your things stolen," he stuttered out.

While I was recovering from this statement he busily set about searching the building for a place for us to spend the night. He selected two small rooms for me to see but one look was enough, for both of them seemed to be already overloaded with tenants, scorpions and spiders.

I returned to Keith and then set about getting the scooter into the grounds of the Administration building and finding somewhere to camp. We made camp under a tree, then locked most of our gear away inside the main office, leaving only our sleeping bags and the scooter outside. As an extra precaution, Keith put the machete beside him.

We did not get much sleep that night because of noise, for down in the canal adjacent to our camp there seemed to be a full-scale gang war in progress.

I woke at the crack of dawn to find brown faces staring down at us. But I ignored them as I got out of my sleeping bag and dressed, then headed for the canal to wash, leaving Keith to slumber on, clutching the machete. I walked to the bridge and in the early morning light was able to see the cause of the night's pandemonium.

The canal was crammed with dozens of craft, everything from tall bowed boats to bamboo rafts. Many of the boats had their sails torn and as I looked closer I could see the reason for the feud. The barges were jockeying for positions to get into the lock which would allow them to enter the main stream to unload and pick up cargo for the return voyage. Most of the barges were heavily laden with cargoes of timber, cows and grain, and no one was giving any quarter as the crews battled physically and verbally for positions. Several fights broke out, as the crew from one boat would pirate another, tossing the defenders overboard.

I had my wash watched by a large number of big grey monkeys, two of whom studied me most intently, ape-ing my movements.

"What are you looking at?"

Displaying their buckteeth, the leering mimics delivered an emphatic lecture on hygiene. Fortunately I could not understand.

After breakfast, we bought our permit, and joined the truck convoy. I was not looking forward to the drive over the spillways as each one was over a mile long and coated with oily slime over the top of which several inches of water ran. If we skidded we had a more than even chance of going over the top and into the river below, but I decided to give it a go and ride in the wake of the truck's duals.

At the sound of a bell the barrier was dropped. The race was on. There were two trucks ahead of me and I kept hard on their tail as they started grinding in low gear onto the first of the weirs. There, I eased the scooter down behind them and onto the greasy spillway.

What we had been told had been no exaggeration, for the surface was inches thick with green oily slime which squelched out from under the truck wheels, leaving me only a narrow strip to ride in. On our left, about three feet away, was a six feet high spillway with water pouring across the road and over the bottom spillway. If we should get out of the wheel tracks there was only five feet between us and the river. I kept close behind in the wake of the trucks, not taking my eyes off the narrow strip. We were wet with spray when we climbed the opposite bank with only three weirs to go.

The second crossing was not too bad as it was a little drier, but the third one was a battle from the word go. Soon my boots and socks were full of slime, for I had to use my legs as stabilisers.

Within the last fifty yards on the fourth and final crossing we had a first class spill. The slime was three inches thick right across the road in this section, and when we hit it, the scooter shot over on to the left side and skated along its steel panniers with me trying to swing it round to stop it going into the river.

Keith could do little with one arm in plaster, so he made a quick dismount and left me to it.

I finally bulldogged the machine across the spillway to a slimy halt. It was hard to stand but somehow we got the machine back on to its wheels and eased it across the last of the mire on to dry earth.

"Phew!" I breathed a big sigh of relief as we climbed the hill on the other side and looked back at our conquest.

The country now became flat, with sugar cane growing as far as the eye could see. When we left the cane fields we entered open forest country amongst which small villages were scattered. The huts in these villages were different from the south as they were of a conical construction and made of palm leaves. The villagers themselves seemed different, cleaner and healthier looking – and not as deaf as their southern brothers. The sun was setting as we pulled up in front of a modern looking hotel in the colourful city of Vishakhapatnam. This hotel had been recommended as the best eating house in the city but it reminded me of a saloon bar in a Wild West frontier towns minus the hitching rails, but of course, with plenty of Indians!

In the crowded smoky dining room we sat down at a table. A waiter handed us a menu written in Hindi. Very helpful! A hungry looking Indian was gorging an omelette, which did not look too bad, so pointing at the omelette we ordered two each. An English-speaking waiter appeared out of the smoke,

"Would you like to wash before dinner, Sirs?" he asked.

Thinking this was a joke we followed him to a door which he opened for us. It was a washroom alright, and we made the most of it.

We bought some fruit and chappatis for breakfast and rode out of town but before long the motor cut out – dirty petrol again. I managed to get to a badly lit garage where I set about cleaning out the fuel line amidst a curious crowd that packed in about me. In the near darkness, I made the silly mistake of winding the throttle cable out too far and, not aware of this, started the motor.

What a shock I got when the machine went berserk and burst through the crowd, terrorising the locals, and roared off into the night with me draped across the handlebars. Having no clutch, the fluid drive had put the machine into full flight. The only apparent damage seemed to be the back of my leg, where I had dragged it across the air filter, taking off a layer of skin. Having fixed the machine, we left to find a campsite.

Waking at daybreak, we found a large group of villagers already gathered around and staring silently at us. We ate a breakfast of tinned meat and drank tea, still watched by the silent audience. I was feeling a little frisky this morning and decided to give our admirers a display in packing up.

First I showed them my sleeping bag, holding it up in one hand, while in the other I held its cover. Then I indicated that I was going to put the big one into the smaller one, and proceeded to stuff the sleeping bag into its cover. As it disappeared, I was applauded by cheers and "Oohs" and "Aahs" from my audience.

I had made a hit!

Keith's spirit stove also had them intrigued and they edged their way closer, trying to get a better look. They were curious and polite, but a nuisance, as they refused to move out of our way when we wanted to get at the scooter. We tried almost everything to get them to shift but with no success. Finally in desperation, I unsheathed the machete, waved it in the air and let out a blood-curdling scream.

I obtained the desired effect. Of the now wary crowd only three typically curious children edged their way close to us again. We had overstayed our welcome so I bounced the scooter back on to the road and away we went to tackle the new day.

Now we were riding through mile after mile of citrus orchards. A festival was being celebrated at the larger villages, and we passed crowds of people, colourfully dressed in green, yellow, mauve and red silk and cotton garments. Drummers preceded the groups, chanting as they beat their three feet long drums, while behind them the headman walked in the shade of an umbrella held by an attendant.

Long lines of women carrying huge baskets full of bananas, oranges, coconuts and other fruit on their heads amazed us, for most of them must have walked at least fifteen miles with these baskets, with nothing more than a ring pad on their heads.

One village sported a colourfully decorated fairground where happy, milling people enjoyed themselves to the accompaniment of loud speakers blaring Hindu music. Still further north we passed a few villages that specialised in animal auctions, selling droves of cattle, donkeys, elephants, horses, goats and even monkeys.

As we skirted Lake Chilka on the coast, I felt something odd was happening but we had to drive several miles before I realised what it was. The people and the animals were shifting off the road when I blew the horn, something that had not happened since leaving Australia. This convinced me that the peoples of the south were either deaf or bone-lazy.

CHAPTER THREE

The next three days were to be a battle with the road to Calcutta. Ahead of us were unknown river crossings which the A.A. had warned us were impassable. The alternative was a detour inland, adding another five hundred miles on to our route, but being only three hundred miles from Calcutta, we decided to tackle the horror stretch.

Twenty miles beyond our campsite we came to our first ferry. With Keith walking beside me I drove down the steep, muddy approach to the bamboo raft ferry and was startled to see a gleaming new Mercedes Benz waiting to board the raft. Standing beside the car was a worried white woman and three Indians. The wife of the German Consul in Calcutta had been touring Eastern India and was now on her way back via the Coast Road. As I glanced at the almost new car I could see a number of telltale battle scars of encounters with rough roads and ferry crossings.

The deck of the raft was strewn with junk and after driving the scooter across a narrow plank onto the deck I had to play hopscotch to get the machine into a spot allocated to me. With the aid of the lady's chauffeur, we bargained for a price to take us over, saving ourselves a few rupees as a result.

The chauffeur started the car and crept forward onto the two narrow planks. As the front wheels landed on the deck of the raft it gave a violent lurch and I made a dive for the scooter and hung on hard, expecting it to tumble into the river. The raft gradually righted itself and nearly submerged as the car was positioned with the front and back of it hanging over the edge of the gunnels, making it impossible to walk the length of the raft without passing through the car, but this did not worry the crew members.

Our vessel was all but under water and when the long bamboo pole was used to propel us the decks became awash. None of the passengers dared move but the crew treated the situation as just another crossing. ... ...

We were having a lunch of coconuts when a Land Rover pulled up and a Bengali in white jumped out.

"The name's Monty. I was working down the road with my survey gang when I saw you go past. We don't see many travellers in this area and I thought you may be lost."

"No, we're not lost yet," Keith said.

"What's the road junction ahead?" I asked.

"That," said Monty, "is what I wanted to tell you. The road to the left is the best one to Calcutta while the other is direct, rough and with river crossings, and inadvisable, as you have the Hoogly river to cross. If you must go that way, find the Chief Engineer of the construction of the new bridge to be built across the Hoogly and tell him I sent you. If you don't see him you have no chance and will be forced to return."

"I'm glad you came along," Keith said.

"Yes, thanks a lot," I added.

He and his assistant climbed back into the Land Rover, and with a wave and a blast of the horn tore off down the road in a cloud of dust. Refreshed, we moved out to tackle the notorious Coast Road.

We camped that night in a dried up paddy field, sleeping between the contours.

As we had forgotten to put the sterilising tablets in the water bags the night before we had to boil the billy next morning. This meant a timber chase, walking round the fields picking up every skerick of grass or twig we could find. Lighting a fire anywhere in India was a major problem and this place was no exception.

While the billy was boiling, I noticed a native busy in the adjoining field with a primitive plough pulled by two white oxen. Deciding to take a photo, I started off towards the workers.

I was within thirty yards of them when the boy suddenly looked up and spotted me and jerked the oxen to a halt. He froze on the spot as I approached. As I lifted the camera he took off in a cloud of dust as though the Devil himself was after him and hid amongst some trees on the other side of the field.

Only then did I realise how frightening I must have looked with my stringy beard and mop of uncombed hair and the Devil Box in my hands. I was determined to get a photo so I lay in ambush behind one of the earth walls which ringed the paddy field. A few minutes later the boy came creeping back from his hiding place, cautiously looking about to make sure I had gone. He took the handles of the plough, which was no more than a twisted tree stump, and started the oxen moving.

Seeing my chance, I half stood up to take a photo when suddenly he spotted me again and literally flew across the ground, except for a couple of occasions when he fell into some deep furrows. The last I saw of him he was heading like Mercury toward his village, so I took a photo of his oxen and plough.

When I returned to camp Keith chided me for terrorising the natives!

*****

Between the broad sandy banks of the river were the remains of a wooden bridge which had been washed away in one of the mighty monsoon seasons. Now all that remained was a string of piles twisted like short spaghetti. The total width of the river was over four hundred yards, about two hundred of which was water and the rest soft sand which we would have to drive through. There was no apparent sign of a road on the opposite bank and, if our friend Monty was correct, this crossing would really keep us busy.

We left the scooter at the top of the bank and walked down to see the ferrymen. They were wild looking and very black-skinned, but one of them could speak a little English and we asked him how much to go across. He consulted his mates, then held up his two hands with fingers and thumbs outstretched, and barked out, "Rupees."

We objected to the price in our most hurt tone of voice and commenced bargaining with them, waving our arms about and gesticulating violently. Finally we got them down to four rupees. We were considering this offer when we remembered Monty had told us of another crossing further upstream. So leaving the ferrymen to wonder what was happening we set off in search of the other crossing.

However, we could not find it and decided to give it away before we ran out of petrol and get back to our ferry.

We were greeted by a leer from the ferry man, as though to say, we knew you'd be back.

"Is four rupees still the price to cross," I asked.

"Yes, Sahib," (very politely).

This looked too easy, and I was waiting for the catch, but nothing happened, so we loaded the scooter onto the boat.

The vessel was a shallow-keeled, poorly constructed boat propelled by a large flat paddle shaped like a tennis racquet, churned in the water in a half circular movement by two coolies. We cast off and drifted out from the shore before the paddle took over.

When we got into midstream the boat stopped and the skipper came forward and with an evil grin on his face demanded eight rupees to finish the crossing.

"No," we said firmly. "We settled for four, and that's all you're getting."

As if by command the boat suddenly started to drift downstream and it was obvious that if we did not pay up we would finish in the Bay of Bengal. I had a go at bargaining again and offered him six to take us in. While we were arguing the boat had drifted on to a sandbar and now all hands were trying to push the boat clear with long bamboo poles. They heaved the boat clear from the bar but in doing so pushed it into an inner channel which ran in quite close to the sandy beach.

Sensing victory, I took up the battle again.

"You have wronged us," I told the skipper, "if you do not take the four rupees you will be stuck again."

His hawk eyes surveyed us for a few seconds and with a hurt expression on his face he said he would accept.

We had won the day but we were not yet off the boat.

Keith, with his plastered arm, waded ashore and waited for the delivery, while I stood in the cool crystal water and supervised the unloading. The scooter was inched down the plank then through the water on to the hard yellow sand. I felt relieved to get it ashore and willingly paid the skipper his four rupees.

All I had to do now was ride the scooter across two hundred yards of soft white sand to what seemed the beginning of the road. So, leaving Keith to follow and give me a push if I got stuck, I set off.

Sand showered from the back wheel as it chewed and spun through the soft surface. Battling every inch of the way to keep the machine upright, I eventually reached a five feet high embankment which I had to climb to get on to the road. I gave the scooter all it had – and was half way up when the machine slewed on the bank, tossing me off and pinning me underneath, burying me in the sand.

Refreshed, we saddled up and got under way along a road that was badly potholed and crossed with large, exposed tree roots, but after the sand, it felt like a highway. We passed through swampy country and the road grew worse and became almost impassable for about twenty miles.

At four o'clock we drove into the smelly town of Kolaghat, on the banks of the mighty Hooghly river, the western most branch of the enormous Ganges Delta. Some Hindus believe that the Hooghly is the true outlet for the Ganges.

I was weaving our way through the multitude when we collided with a cycle rickshaw, ripping my rucksack off its frame and bending the rear wheel of the rickshaw inwards. I had barely stopped when the rickshaw driver jumped off his cycle and lunged at me in a tantrum, screaming is Bengali. I ignored him and dismounted to survey the damage but when I saw the state of my rucksack I too, was upset. He was busy shaking his fist in my face when I grabbed him and shook him. He reeled back, eyes popping as he took refuge behind his rickshaw while his passenger shouted abuse at him as well. I made quick repairs, for a mob was gathering around us fast, and we lost no time in getting on the move before trouble flared up.

Our first thoughts were that we would have to be careful with food in Kolaghat, for the place was extremely filthy. Flies were in swarms. After making enquiries we found our way to the office of the Chief Engineer. As I pulled up in front of the building, we were surrounded by a pack of dirty, rough-looking locals who packed in tight to stare at the new arrivals. I asked for the Engineer, but got no response from the silent mob. They stared with cold, lifeless eyes. Suddenly two tall youths, dressed in sarongs and long white shirts pushed their way through the crowd.

"For whom are you looking?" they greeted us.

When we had recovered from the shock of hearing an English-speaking voice, we explained what we wanted. One of then dashed into the office, and five minutes later returned to tell us the Engineer was at dinner but he would see us in an hour's time.

We had not walked one hundred yards before we had a crowd of over two hundred trailing us and whenever we stopped they would close in around us. At times it was impossible to move without walking into or on top of somebody and it appeared as though the whole town was turning out to look at the strangers. The Calcutta student with whom I became friendly introduced himself as Binenona and as we walked he told me about himself and asked questions about Australia.

The town was far from being a tourist resort. On one side of the street stood a few respectable dwellings but the majority were a shambles of mud, wood and bamboo, decaying in the dust. The tall, stark trees lining the river bank were perches for dozens of hideous looking vultures, patiently waiting to feed on carcasses below while their carrion crow playmates squarked their way across the sky and along the slimy river bank.

Mongrel dogs fought the vultures and crows for possession of the rotting carcasses and garbage littered on the bank, which filled the air with its overpowering stench. The river itself was about a mile wide with a thin line of a railway bridge spanning it half a mile downstream.

Binenona asked if I would like to visit the school. I nodded quickly - anything for a change of air. He led us down a narrow alleyway towards the school buildings and climbed through a hole in the wall which brought us into the school yard. We were shown over the new building, introduced to the Principal and some of the teachers and taken to their quarters which were no more than shacks, lit by hurricane lamps and furnished with boxes for tables and a haystack for a bed. The only resemblance to a teacher's quarters was the display of books packed in boxes by the beds. The thought crossed my mind that these teachers must have loved their work to stay here - for I could not imagine many educated people living under these conditions for the poor salary they receive.

It was time to meet the Engineer so we returned to the office, where we were ushered in through a curious crowd packed around the door. The Chief, dressed in whites and looking like an advertisement for soap powders, welcomed us and invited us to tell our story. It was obvious we would have to impress him if we were to cross the river so I set out to do just that. He became very interested, and after a little thought said that we would be given the best of attention and would be ferried across the river, without charge, as soon as the tide was right in the morning.

He showed us to an open-air roadside restaurant, lit by hurricane lamps which glowed a dull yellow in the dust haze. On our arrival a radio was playing moderately to entertain the customers, but hardly had we seated ourselves when the proprietor, thinking we were deaf, turned it up full blast. The loud speaker, which hung outside the door of the kitchen, threw a fit as it vibrated violently against the wall. We were no more than ten feet from the monster and first our ears went numb from the noise, then bells started ringing in our heads. Our friends did not appear to notice the noise, but casually sat and talked – at least I think they were talking! I could see their lips moving! I leaned over and touched Binenona on the arm and pointed at the speaker and then screwed my face up, holding my hands over my ears. He got the message and went to quell the disturbance. After five minutes, the noise was reduced to half volume. The relief on the ears was wonderful and for the first time I listened to the music.

"What's the music all about?" I asked.

"It's about a man running off with another man's wife," he replied.

I listened to the music again. This seemed logical.

After much trouble the boys found us accommodation in a windowless, nine feet square, mud hut.

"Take everything in with you and be sure to bar the door securely or you will end up in the river."

Binenona had told us it would be after ten next morning before we could make the crossing. The tide would not be right until then. We ate a breakfast of sweetmeats, biscuits and tea and left the scooter under the watchful eye of one of the students while we took a walk through the marshalling yards towards the railway bridge where we were greeted by squawking crows and vultures circling over the carcass of a goat. Packs of dogs were staking their claim, fighting off the huge vultures as they swept low, striking at the dogs with their cruel talons. We moved on holding our breath when possible to stop our stomachs from heaving. After passing several more vulture-covered corpses, one of which was human, we had had enough.

With Keith giving me limited assistance with his one arm, I had my hands full to get the scooter down the steep, slimy, muddy banks onto the ferry. Several times I narrowly missed mud dunkings as the machine got out of control and slipped towards the river.

This ferry was an up-to-date model with twin army pontoon floats lashed four feet apart with heavy planking. Dangling over the back was an outboard motor which looked more like an eggbeater. The raft was poled out from the shore, which was now lined with crowds of people waving and cheering as we drifted out from the sordid riverbank. The outboard motor roared into life.

We eventually drew abreast of a few pylons and tangled beams which were once a jetty. On shore, a work force of about forty men was busy around a steam-driven pile driver, which was hammering wooden piles into the soft sand. The raft was moored to two of the stouter pylons and preparations got under way for unloading the scooter.

This meant building a bridge. The loincloth-clad coolies were recruited for the bridge building, and in no time they were busy laying beams and shifting sleepers to make a roadway for us. After an hour's toil in the blazing sun the crude bridge was ready for us; the scooter was hoisted bodily onto the jetty and wheeled across the shaky structure with its mobile planking. When the machine was landed, it had a flat tyre. But we were not allowed to touch it as three men were appointed to fix it. When all was ready we thanked everyone for their help and I handed out pencils which I had been carrying for such an occasion, then we waved goodbye and set off.

Typical East Coast Village

'This ferry was an up-to-date model, with twin army-platoon floats ... '
(Crossing of the Hoogly)

Hindu Temple

'Only three typically-curious children returned ... '

'If we did not pay, we would finish in the Bay of Bengal ... '

Winnowing grain on the road — South India

In Calcutta our first task was to look for the hostel, the address of which we had been given in Madras. It turned out that the building was now a college but the Principal agreed to let us stay provided we made do with the tables and forms in the common room.

"Anywhere", I thought, "so long as I can lie down and rest my heaving stomach." I was suffering from a dysentery attack brought on by the food we had eaten at Kolaghat.

We unpacked our gear and took over a corner of the common room. While Keith went to do some washing and take a bath, I swallowed two dysentery pills and took a sleep. Later, I staggered off to the bathroom to take a plunge and wash my clothes, Calcutta style. I shivered as I up-ended brass urns filled with cold water from a large pond in the middle of the room.

In the evening we strolled out into the crowded street which, we were told, contained two million people. We came to a small café, which seemed clean, so we entered. Keith ordered up big while I, after much negotiating, finally got the cook to make me two slices of toast, probably the first ever made in that café. While we were eating, an English-speaking Bengali came and sat with us and asked us where we came from. On hearing we were Australians, he gave a cheer and proceeded to tell us Australia was a land of cricket, swimming, football and dairy cows. We had a battle trying to get away from our knowledgeable friend, who followed us into the street and dogged us for a block before we lost him.

Next morning we went to the A.A. to get information on the road to Darjeeling and Nepal. They asked us to call back the next day, as most of the information would have to be collected for us. So we rode off to explore the modern part of the city with broad, clean streets and beautiful parklands and gardens, very different to the areas we had already seen.

We decided to dine regally in one of the fashionable restaurants where a doorman in a white uniform was on duty. He eyed us with suspicion, as we bade him "Good morning" and entered the air-conditioned restaurant. Inside, a little man reluctantly showed us a table for two, and acted as though he expected us to steal all the silver. Well-dressed people of many races and colours were dining by candlelight to the accompaniment of a five-piece orchestra, while at the next table sat a party of turbaned and bearded Sikhs and their beautifully dressed wives. On being handed a menu we ordered steak and eggs, determined to get a good meal in preparation for the coming assault on Darjeeling.

Feeling a little healthier, we rode off to the Nepalese Consulate to see about our visas. Leaving our crash helmets on the scooter we entered the beautifully timbered foyer of the building. The place was like a morgue. I was in process of peeking behind some intricately patterned tapestry which was hanging over a door when a little brown man popped out.

"Do you want something?" he enquired.

"Yes, two visas for Nepal."

We presented him with our passports, which he took and disappeared again behind the screen.

Fifteen minutes later he reappeared and courteously conducted us to a reception room with small writing tables scattered about. We were given our passports and a pile of forms to fill in. When completed, we handed them back to him with two passport photos and ten rupees, then he disappeared again, this time for a good hour.

Just as we were beginning to wonder if we were ever going to get our passports back he returned with them in his hand and invited us to ask him any questions we had about his country. Before we had left the Consulate, Nepal was becoming an even more mysterious place in our eyes, thanks to the little man.

Most of next day was spent tourist fashion seeing the sights, including the Black Hole of Calcutta, before winding our way back to the A.A. to collect a most uncertain bundle of information on the routes north to Darjeeling and Katmundu.

CHAPTER FOUR

The next day was Thursday, 2 March. "Holi Day" - the Hindu Festival of Water.

The Water Festival is described in the travel posters as a time for singing, dancing and good humour, and has been handed down from medieval times when an Indian Princess threw rose water over a prince. Unfortunately, over the centuries the custom has got out of hand and now the males drink Bhang, an intoxicant and narcotic made from hemp, and throw anything but rose water. The Principal suggested we stay in the college until midday (when the throwing is supposed to cease) but after talking it over we decided to give it a go.

We were packed and on the road by six-thirty, hoping to get well clear of the city before the festivities started. As we cruised on to the open road and through a small village we got our first glimpse of what the festival meant. We saw several groups of people throwing red and green, yellow and black coloured water over each other and using pint sized squirt guns with great accuracy. We, of course, thought this very amusing, not realising that our turn was to come.

Three hours later we found ourselves in the thick of it, running gauntlet after gauntlet and receiving great doses of coloured liquids. I tried stopping away from the mobs (already dressed for the part in homespun cotton, baggy, white pyjamas), but we were assaulted just the same by dozens of people who would race up to us with squirt guns and buckets of ochre in an attempt to smother and drown us. Quick getaways were necessary in order to survive and at times I found myself driving dangerously, almost running over inebriated, glazed-eyed locals. On several occasions my vision was completely blurred as coloured water ran over my goggles and mixed with purple and green powder on my face. We intended stopping but there seemed to be no place of refuge, for even on the open road a crowd would be lying in wait for the unwary traveller. By this time I was sporting a red face and green beard, and, to stop our clothes becoming even more stained, we donned our raincoats.

Further north we were pelted with paper water bombs, often managing to dodge them as they were hurled through the air from a distance.

The worst was still to come. Along what seemed to be a quiet stretch of road we were attacked by a crowd armed with paint brushes on long sticks and carrying great pots of paint (with silver frost the favourite colour). There was little we could do to escape.

We rode on until midday, when we found a shady spot by a buffalo wallow and had a cleanup in the muddy water. After an hour's spell we got going again as we wished to reach the Ganges that evening.

According to the rules the water throwing was to stop at midday, and since it was now after one o'clock we moved off feeling reasonably safe.

I was sitting on a steady fifty miles an hour on a good stretch of road when, WHOP! I saw stars as something hit me on the right temple, almost knocking me off the scooter and causing a spill. I wavered and screeched to a halt, to discover that a youth had thrown a big clod of sodden paper about the size of a cricket ball at me. I was furious and looked around just in time to see the culprit making a dash for it across the fields as fast as his legs could carry him. We had had a close escape, for a little farther to the front and I would have got it in the eyes. As it was, my goggles were broken.

When I had regained my composure, we set off again to the Ganges.

The road worsened until it was nothing more than a narrow gutter of fine, white dust. The day was hot and dry and occasionally we had to bulldoze the "Rabbit" through thick mud as the road crossed a series of paddy fields in which coolies had been working until we arrived on the scene.

We passed the point of no return when we came upon a road construction gang busily engaged in laying red bricks for the foundations of a new road. Our speed dropped to almost nil as Keith had to walk ahead clearing a path through the bricks while I bounced the scooter along behind. The whole operation was watched by unhelpful workers, who stood like statues, staring at us with marble expressions.

We battled our way over the bricks, then came to a bitumen road and for the first time that day we were able to relax on the peaceful road.

Just on sunset I spotted a muddy buffalo wallow and decided to replenish our water supply and have a wash while we had the opportunity. The water was a dirty grey colour and we put in a double dose of sterilising tablets to make sure.

Refreshed, we rode off along a road that occasionally disappeared in gullies covered in thick dust before we arrived at the village of Dkuiban on the banks of the river Ganges.

Next morning, we found that the villagers were still suffering the aftermath of the previous day's Water Festival. Practically everyone and everything was splattered with colourful dyes. Several times we were almost attacked by glassy eyed inebriates, who staggered about the place causing havoc where they could.

Several Sikh truck drivers were fussing over their big Mercedes trucks while they waited to board the ferry.

Leaving Keith in the company of some white-bearded elders

and the scooter, I made for the river to see what else I could learn about the crossing. A young Bengali greeted me in English.

"Do you wish to make the crossing?"

My new found friend was engaged on a road survey for the Shell Petrol Company and busied himself making enquiries for me about the departure times.

To fill in time till the midday ferry left, he offered to show me around the village. As we stopped at a char house, a crowd gathered, including a number of tall, rough-looking Sikhs who cautiously used the Shell Man as an Interpreter as they questioned me. The biggest of them invited us to join them for a meal, so I accepted and went to get Keith.

We sat down in the bamboo char house and were given a large bowl of curried rice and freshly made dark brown chappatis from the dung fire. The Sikhs sat opposite, surveying us with their dark eyes and smirking as we fumbled the goo awkwardly into our mouths. One of them, demonstrating, suggested that we use the chappatis as a shovel. The curry was burning hot and between each mouthful I gulped down large quantities of water to quell the furnace in my stomach.

Sweating profusely, we thanked the Sikhs for the meals then walked to the landing stage with the Shell Man to see if the ferry had arrived.

It had, and for the first time we had something solid – a converted landing craft. The waiting trucks of our Sikh friends rolled on and I followed with Mirrabooka.

Nobody seemed to be in a hurry, for the crew and the truck drivers stripped to the waist and took a plunge into the Ganges, wallowing around in the murky water. The tough looking Sikhs decided to wash their hair, and on taking off their turbans, disclosed their long black plaits, making the big fellows look like overgrown schoolgirls. A bystander presented Keith and I with a bottle of sacred Ganges water to take with us to cure all ills.

When the stars of the show had had their baths, everyone scrambled aboard and the big diesel engines throbbed into life. The barge backed away from the muddy bank to face upstream and everyone settled themselves in a cool spot for the voyage. The truck crews were perched on top of their high loads to get the full advantage of the breeze.

The peaceful atmosphere was disturbed occasionally by a celebrating, middle aged, dye-stained Bengali still suffering a hangover from the Water Festival.

The barge churned along close to the high banks, giving us a closer look at the villages, which have to be rebuilt after every monsoon. Flights of sun-baked mud steps led down to the river where platforms had been built to enable the villagers to wash and draw water. Women carrying huge water urns on their heads staggered up these steep steps while the men bathed and mended fishing nets.

Moored close by the mud platforms were dozens of fishing boats, most seeming ready to fall apart. Awkward looking vessels with flat bottoms, pear shaped rudders and tall, curved bamboo masts, they looked top heavy and possibly easy to capsize. No doubt they had been built this way to negotiate the numerous sandbars which clog the river in the dry season.

On the riverbank, forests of bamboo were being worked by the villagers who were cutting the best of the sticks and tossing them into the river. There they were rafted and floated downstream to be marketed.

Further upstream we passed white-robed women pounding their washing on flat rocks, making a din that echoed off the high mud banks.

As the LST swung into midstream we passed an anchored fishing boat from which came the high pitched wail of voices. The crew was Muslim and their muezzin was leading them in prayer.

By the time we reached midstream, it was impossible to see either bank and the only thing that broke the monotony was an old paddle-wheeler which passed us pouring black smoke from its lofty funnel and blotting out the sun. She had just had a facelift and was freshly painted, all the colours of the rainbow.

With scenery gone for the present, I turned my attentions to the Sikhs who had now moved alongside us. Again using the Shell Man as interpreter, they began questioning us about our destination, trying to make us believe they knew no English. The pretence proved too much for them, and they finally broke down and spoke to us in English, explaining that they liked to have a joke.

The big men were concerned about our welfare. They kept asking what we ate and when, and where we slept.

"We eat where we can and sleep under the stars," I said.

This seemed to upset them, as they shook their heads and replied,

"That won't do. You'll have your throats cut."

"Where are you sleeping tonight?" asked one.

Silently, I shrugged my shoulders.

The smaller of our two companions then went below onto the main deck to hold a meeting of the Sikh drivers. After five minutes talking he returned.

"We would consider it a pleasure if you would travel with us to Siliguri. You will be our guests along the road."

Keith and I felt honoured and thanked them.

The remainder of the voyage was spent in easy conversation with the Sikhs.

"You have been lucky to make such good friends," the Shell Man told me on the quiet.

Four hours after our departure, a small village on the northern bank turned out to be our landing stage and the beginning of the road. As the barge was being moored I surveyed the road we would have to travel. It was no more than a track across white sand-hills, with steel matting laid on the uphill sections.

The big trucks rolled off the barge and were parked beside a flimsy char house, then the Sikhs invited us to join them in a cup of tea. While we were drinking, some of the villagers tried souveniring our crash helmets, but they barely cleared the hut before they were pulled down by the Sikhs and roughed up for pilfering.

One of the Sikhs tried to persuade us to put the machine on top of his truck, but owing to the height, it was out of the question. Instead we were placed No.3 in the convoy (so that we would not get lost) and were given instructions to stop if we wanted anything. This was all very well until we started crossing the sand-hills and found ourselves eating the dust of the trucks ahead. However, after five miles we came to a battered bitumen road and at least lost the dust.

It was nearly sunset when we arrived in Malda and joined the Sikhs at a char house, to find them waiting for us with a meal of curry and chapattis.

We pulled out in the last of the twilight and ran down a steep embankment on to one of the most primitive pontoon bridges I have ever seen. It was like a scenic railway decked with bark and steel matting – and the ride across was about as hair raising.

The road from here on was fair bitumen and we kept a steady pace in the convoy. Now and then a truck would cruise up beside us and a bearded head would poke out of the window and shout, "Are you alright? Do you need rest?"

At a road junction near Bapsel, close to the East Pakistan border, we were flagged down by the truckies, who were standing round their vehicles taking refreshments. We were each offered a large glass of water-like liquid and some chappati. We were curious about the liquid; for something without either taste or smell it was certainly being handled reverently.

"Drink up. It will do you good," encouraged one of the Sikhs with a rather pained expression. We could not offend him. Keith emptied his glass and had it topped up again.

"How do you like it?"

Keith hesitated for a moment, then, earnestly,
"Quite good. It is very smooth."
Then turning aside he whispered in my ear,
"Tastes like flaming water to me."
Before we moved off the big Sikh leader stepped forward.
"Stay with us," he said, "I know of a place where you can sleep the night."
"Thanks," and we rode off in the convoy again.

We had travelled about ten miles when a strange sensation started to creep over me. My hands were going numb and I could not feel the handlebars. "Circulation must have stopped," I thought, "must be holding the handlebars too tight."

I was in the process of restoring life to my arms by shaking them when my feet and legs went the same way. I stamped my feet on the floorboards but it was no use. Suddenly Keith burst into song and slumped forward now and then, resting on my back.

It was then that I realised that we were both intoxicated.

As I peered ahead at the tail-light of the truck, determined not to lose it, a loud buzzing sensation started inside my head. Then a whole battalion of little men with jackhammers marched between my ears and a great nausea swept over me, numbing my body. I fought to keep my eyes open and started talking, telling myself that I was not going to sleep.

I throttled down and looked at the speedo – but was startled to see at least six of them. I concentrated on the middle one and watched one of the needles fall to 20 mph. If we were going to have a crash it would be slow.

Driving through native villages, I could see thousands of beautifully coloured orange lights, which in reality were rows of hurricane lamps lining the street. The lights did not bother me too much, but the people walking across the road did. I remember slowing down to drive between dozens of people walking in every direction. I dodged the thickest apparitions and apparently did not hit anybody. Blaring village radios, screeching Hindu music took the last vestige of reality from me.

For the next ten or twenty miles, I am not exactly sure what happened. It was like a dream, except that I remember telling myself to keep awake and not to go too fast.

After an unknown time I broke out in a cold sweat, and the body gradually came back to normal as the cool night air revived me. It had been an unforgettable experience. I was pleased to find that Keith was still with me and I called out to him.

"Okay now," he answered, "but a while ago I was floating along at a terrific speed. It was beaut!"

We eventually caught up with the trucks, which had got well-ahead of us during our blackout period. They were pulled up off the road beside a group of mud huts and I cruised in behind them and parked. The Sikh who had given us the drink came over to greet us. I was determined not to let him see we had been affected by the brew, and I walked forward to meet him bracing myself in case my knees collapsed. Keith was in the same condition and I had to smile as he stepped high over small pebbles.

"You feel like a sleep?" the Sikh began.

"Not in the least," I cut in.

"What was the drink you gave us?" asked Keith.

"Rice wine. Did you like it? It is a special for us drivers."

"I thought you Sikhs were not allowed to drink," I said.

The big fellow grinned. "Just a little. It keeps us strong. You too must be strong to take what you did."

Keith and I shook our heads and tried to look tough as we swayed in the breeze.

We were introduced to the owner of the char house, a wiry, hawk-eyed Bengali. The Sikhs had obviously asked if we could stay the night and the owner had agreed but had insisted on payment in advance. The biggest of the Sikhs gave him a few rupees and stopped us digging in our pockets. The question of food was raised and we were asked what we would like for breakfast. Eggs sounded pretty safe so we ordered them.

When the Sikh delivered our order, the owner threw in an objection, asking for more money. The big, bearded fellow exploded and started shouting and abusing the owner in Bengali. The latter in turn protested, waving his arms in the air and returning the abuse. At this the big fellow really went off the handle and picked up the Bengali by the shoulders and shook him until I thought his eyes would pop out of his head. The Bengali screamed surrender and the Sikh put him down. He stood there for a few moments, vibrating from the shaking he had taken. The big fellow casually turned to us and said,

"He has agreed to feed you two meals, one now and one in the morning. Give him no money."

I was beginning to believe that the Sikhs were a truly warlike race ... ...

We stumbled through a too-small, mud doorway and entered a large back room where there was a raised mud platform for a bed.

"This is your room." A voice told us from out of the dark.

A boy entered with a hurricane lamp. The Sikhs and their truck crews got busy giving the place a spring-clean, tossing everything out that they considered in the way. I felt sorry for the owner and asked them to take it easy. This, however, had the reverse effect and they made up brooms to sweep the place out.

When all was ready, we had our gear brought into the room for us and Mirrabooka placed in the foyer.

Then we all retired to the char house and sat talking by the dung fire until the tea ran out and the Sikhs said they had better be on the road.

"Don't forget to call in on us at Siliguri in the morning and let us know how the Bengali treated you," they added.

I gathered that if we gave them an adverse report on the Bengali they would take the place apart on the next trip. We thanked them for their help, shook hands and gave them a wave as they drove off, giving final instructions to our newly subdued motel owner.

Keith and I retired to our kennel and settled down for the night. I was just dozing off when outside the front door somebody started singing in a long drawn out mournful wail, which carried on into the night. At regular intervals a chorus of dogs would join in. I had the feeling that the singing was deliberately kept up to keep us awake – but it did not quite succeed.

The country was flat and uninteresting except for two river crossings, which were beauts!

Their approaches were across miles of dust, as fine as talc powder, having been trampled that way by millions of feet over the centuries. This dust in places was up to a foot deep. It covered the floorboards and made driving dangerous as well as being hard on the tyres, for underneath was a collection of sharp rocks capable of slashing tyres to pieces. These two crossings really tested our skill in staying upright.

Near each of them we passed thousands of workers, engaged in bridge construction. They moved in long files, shifting dirt in two feet diameter cane baskets, which were carried on the head. As we passed one long line a few of the workers stopped to stare at us, thus causing a concertina pileup of basket carriers.

On arriving in Siliguri, we decided to try to make Darjeeling by nightfall and not to spend any time in town - even though we had an invitation from our Sikh mates. Darjeeling was only fifty miles away and as far as we knew there was a good road all the way.

The weather was burning hot as we rode across the last of the dry, flat country before the climb. In the hazy distance we could see the dark wall of the Himalayan foothills, on top of which lay a thick blanket of cloud. We had hardly started on the first grade when the scooter coughed and came to a halt. Dirty petrol.

I set about cleaning the filter bowl in the shade of the dense jungle, wherein the tiger, leopard, elephant, deer, bear and rhinoceros had their home. The job was just finished when there came a high pitched whistle and the noise of a puffing engine. We looked around in time to see a small colourful, red engine pulling six toy-like blue trucks and a guards-van along the two feet gauge railway, which runs from Siliguri to Darjeeling. Black smoke poured from the oversize funnel and the engine looked as though it would vibrate off the rails if it went any faster. Nepalese brakemen were riding on top of every carriage ready to spin the bag wheels they were sitting on should the train get out of control on one of the steep grades ... ...

*****

At the three thousand feet mark, we got our first views of some spectacular Himalayan scenery. Although only a preview of things to come, it was still breathtaking with enormous gorges opening out before us and small villages and isolated houses hanging precariously on the edges of ravines as though about to topple over.

We were now entering the tea country and most of the slopes as far as the eye could see were a carpet of patterned tea plantations.

I kept a sharp lookout for trains, as the railway line criss-crossed the road in the most unexpected places, and we never knew when a careering train would cross our path. Twice, I heard a high-pitched whistle and only just managed to stop in time, as a toy train thundered across our path, vibrating the ground as it went.

At 6,000 feet a battered Land Rover came coasting down the range towards us with two Indian boys running alongside, kicking the front wheels every time the vehicle approached a curve. It pulled up in front of us, and a tall, Anglo-Indian chap with an enormous handlebar moustache jumped out.

"Captain Bijanbasi, ex Indian Army. Where the hell do you think you are going on that machine?"

"Darjeeling."

He stroked his moustache. "Got a place to stay there?"

"No. Any suggestions?"

"If I was there you could stay with me, but I won't be. I'll give you the address of a friend. He'll fix you up."

While Keith was writing the address on his plaster cast, I asked the Captain where he was off to.

"Oh, yes, I have a broken tie-rod and I am going down to Siliguri to have it fixed. The tricky part about it is that I have absolutely no steering and have to rely on the boys to kick the front wheels around the curves."

The boys had bare feet and, although they all looked pretty happy at the time, I wondered how many pairs of broken feet there would be at the bottom.

At the crest of our 7,404 feet climb we were almost frozen to the scooter; in fact, my hands were like two blocks of ice. We had intended to stop and dig out our sweaters and long trousers but the sight of Darjeeling through the swirling, dark grey cloud decided us to grit our teeth and make an express run into town.

As we rode through villages on the way, small boys chased us and jumped on the back of the scooter as we passed. One lad tried to jump from an eight feet high wall, but he missed the scooter. At first we were amused at these antics, but it gradually became annoying and sometimes extremely dangerous as the little villains would half mount the tail rack and knock us off balance, sending the scooter careering across the road into the path of oncoming traffic. Whenever we rode through Nepalese villages Keith was forced to ride shotgun and repel the invaders.

Darjeeling appeared to be built on the side of a seven thousand feet mountain and as we drove into the town, we caught glimpses of the narrow streets zigzagging up and down the mountainside. Heavy cloud was now closing in fast and visibility in places was down to yards.

When we dismounted in the town square, we found it almost impossible to stand up and it was some time before I could creak my way over to one of the prettiest cops I have ever seen.

He was one of Darjeeling's stocky Nepalese policemen and

was dressed in a bright blue uniform with shiny silver buttons and red striped trousers. A Chocolate Soldier blue and red striped cap was cocked on one side of his head and, but for the chinstrap, he would have been standing beside it. I stood shivering beside him while he gave a display of whistle blowing and hand signalling. When the traffic eased and he took the whistle out of his mouth, he threw me a snappy salute. We must have looked comical, this five feet of immaculate efficiency and myself, six feet of boots, socks, shorts and wind-cheater topped by a wild black beard and white skid-lid.

"Speak English?" I asked.

"Police," he replied, pointing in the direction of the police station. We asked an English-speaking official if he could direct us to Mr. Avari, showing him the address printed on Keith's plaster cast.

"One moment, I will ring him."

"Yes. He is expecting you now," he said as he hung up.

From the warmth of the police station, we ventured out into the cold mountain air again and driving up the zigzag street, parked before the paint-starved picture theatre. Entering the antique foyer, we asked for Mr. Avari and were shown up a flight of creaking wooden steps to the top floor where the gentleman in question was waiting.

We told him of our meeting with the Captain and of his suggestion that Mr. Avari might be able to get us accommodation.

"What sort of accommodation would you like? I would be delighted to help in any way I can." He produced a list of hotels and rattled off their tariffs.

"Nothing too flash," Keith put in, "so long as it's reasonable with a place to park the scooter."

Mr. Avari paused for a moment, stroking his moustache.

"Ah, I have it."

He picked up the phone and made a call. After an involved discussion he hung up, and leaning back in his chair with a smile on his face, said,

"A friend of mine who owns a second class hotel is going to put you up. He owes me £500 so I think you will be getting the best of attention. If there is anything you want, or if my friend plays up, let me know. I have threatened him with charges if he does."

We thanked him and left, feeling thankful that we had met Captain Bijanbasi, but sorry for our future landlord.

At the hotel doorway we were met by a very nervous little Bengali of Nepalese extraction, with a grey wool cap pulled right down over his ears.

"Messrs Bassett and Ward?"

"That's us," we replied.

"Is it true you are great friends of Mr. Avari?"

"Oh, yes, the greatest," I assured him.

The little man immediately went into action and tried to kill us with service, as three Nepalese boys swept in and took our gear up to our room for us. A space was cleared in the hallway for the scooter, which was carried in and gently placed on the floor. By the time I got to our room he was fussing about the place like a broody hen, arranging furniture and sweeping the floor.

The hotel was not exactly first class but being special guests we had been given the only room that had a window and a door that locked.

"If there is anything at all you want, just call and I will attend to your needs personally," the manager said, pawing us and bowing.

"Could we have a hot bath when we return from our walk?" Keith asked.

"Most certainly."

We rugged up, warm for the first time, set out to appease our Himalayan appetites.

Darjeeling was full of American tourists. Every white face seemed to have an American accent to go with it.

We were plodding our way up a steep hill in the grey twilight when we met three heavily rugged tourists. On closer inspection we discovered that two of them were women. The rimless spectacled man greeted us with,

"Say, which part of the States do you guys came from?"

I got in first. "Queensland." This appeared to rattle him a little and the older of the women eventually said,

"Never heard of the place. Is it part of Texas or one of the other Southern States?"

"No," I said, "it is twice the size of Texas."

By the look on their faces, I doubt if they believed that such a place existed. I was waiting for the next move when the younger woman spoke.

"Are you the two who rode into town this afternoon on a little machine and wearing shorts?"

"How do you like the scenery?" Keith said.

We finally told them we were from Australia, then left these incredulous whirlwind globetrotters to their Tourist Brochures.

Back at the hotel our hot bath was waiting us, so we took it in turn to use the primitive, and seldom-used bathroom, which was on the roof. Breakfast, next morning, was served in bed, in our icebox room.

The alpine air was clean and crisp and visibility was excellent. Without hesitation, we made a beeline for the highest point in

Darjeeling to get our first good views of the Himalayan Range. We were not disappointed. The panoramas were absolutely breathtaking, with a full view of the world's third highest peak, Kangchenjunga, at 28,216 feet, dominating the skyline.

We wandered back through town and out to Birch Hill along the narrow bridle track. With the exception of a few Land Rovers, jeeps and some rattly old buses, there is very little in the way of transport in Darjeeling and even then it is only along a few streets.

Being mountain-lovers, we were anxious to see the recently built Himalayan Mountaineering Institute, located at the end of an isolated ridge amongst birches and silver firs. As we nosed our way around the buildings, one of the staff offered to show us around. We were shown through the library, a study, lecture rooms, workshops, records-room, shown photographs and a special display of mountaineering equipment. This display adjoined a very neatly laid out Himalayan Museum, which dealt with geology, flora and fauna. From the windows of the class room, wonderful panoramic views of the Himalayan Range could be seen.

On our way back to town I was fascinated by the human packhorses. They were tiny Nepalese, almost black from the coal which they were carrying in large cane baskets, supported only by a broad leather band around the forehead.

It was late in the evening by the time we reached our hotel. We were relaxing when we had a visitor, a reporter from the Darjeeling News, who was after a story. In return he offered to get us information on a supposed road between Darjeeling and Katmandu. I had not heard anything of this road but we looked forward with interest to any information available.

Next morning we again visited the Mountaineering Institute where we were lucky enough to meet Tensing, of Everest fame, before going to the office to get details of our proposed walk to Sandak Phu. The fact that we did not want any Sherpas caused an upheaval in the office. Apparently nobody walks in the Himalayas without Sherpas. Feeling boycotted, I asked for a map, but was told that there was none because it was a Military Area. However, I saw a sketch map and at the first opportunity we borrowed a piece of paper and made a tracing.

We officially checked out and went to buy supplies for the trip, handing over unwanted gear to the Manager, who promised to guard it and the scooter with his life.

The first leg of our journey was by bus, to Ghumm. The bus was a converted utility fitted with wooden seats and the best of air conditioning. After we had thrown our rucksacks in and climbed in ourselves there was not much room left. The driver sat patiently behind the steering wheel while the ticket collector raced around the bazaar trying to recruit passengers to make a full load for the trip.

Four passengers climbed on of their own free will but another four were literally dragged onto, and in one case bullied into the bus instead of walking. In a country of habitual walkers, something had to be done to keep the bus line going.

When we had a full load the second-in-command cranked the bus and the engine spluttered into life. The bus had only one gear – flat out. It careered through the bazaar and on to the open road with the ticket collector swinging on the rear step screaming out, "Ghumm bus," at the top of his voice.

The passengers, including ourselves, were a rough looking bunch. Sitting beside Keith was a hefty, broad-shouldered Tibetan colourfully dressed in his native garb of woollen knee boots, grubby tunic and a fur cap with wide ear muffs. In his belt was a long straight dagger, the size of a small sword. His flat Mongol face made him look a tough customer, and I smiled at the contrast between him and my casual, red-bearded mate gazing nonchalantly over the landscape.

At Ghumm we stepped out into a pea soup fog with visibility down to feet. We had the address of a hostel close by, so, feeling our way, we set out. By some strange coincidence, we found the track and started the steep climb, though barely able to see our outstretched hands. The path flattened and we walked straight into a stone wall. Circumnavigating the building we found the door and knocked. It opened and a small boy stood before us. As soon as we spoke he ran off and returned shortly with three teenage boys all of whom could speak English.

"This the Hostel?" we asked.

"Come in out of the cloud. The Hostel has been turned into a school."

It was good to get inside and warm up by the open fire. The Headmaster was brought and told us we could stay the night provided we did not mind sleeping on the floor. "That will do us," we said thankfully.

Bright sunlight was streaming through the window next morning as we thanked our hosts for their hospitality and set off for Pharloot. The boys insisted they accompany us for part of the fifteen-mile walk to Joreporri. Four miles later we felt like Pied Pipers with about twenty boys trotting along with us. Whenever one of them passed a relative's house, he would pay a quick visit and return with biscuits and cups of tea. This kept up for eight miles until the small fry exhausted themselves.

The track led us through a silver fir forest, the floor of which was carpeted with dark-green moss and millions of small, colourful wildflowers. Festoons of cream coloured orchids hung in profusion from the trees. All the way through the forest the sound of running water could be heard as little streams trickled their way across the track.

Joreporri was a village of six mud buildings and about as many wooden ones. Before we could even take our rucksacks off, we were challenged by a Ghurka police sergeant armed with a pistol and Kukri. Without drawing breath he made an earnest speech in his native language and indicated he wanted us to go with him. Two other policemen joined him and we were escorted to the police station. We were bundled inside, and as soon as we were able, dumped our rucksacks on the floor. Four more police were placed on guard by the doors and windows while an officer behind a desk indicated he wanted us to sit.

It had all happened so quickly we scarcely had time to object – not that it would have done us any good.

The scowling officer delivered a lengthy discourse in Nepalese. When he had finished I politely smiled at him.

"Speak English?" I said and digging out my passport, I handed it to him. Keith handed his over also and we sat back to await the next move. The officer burst into more dialogue, the only word I could understand being 'Russian'. It looked as though we had been picked up as Russian spies. We moved over to the desk and tried explaining that we were Australians, using our passports to try and make him understand.

A seesaw conversation broke out in two languages with an eight-to-two majority against us. This business of crossing the border was something about which the Mountaineering Institute had not told us.

To make matters worse, our visa for Nepal was stamped via Amlekhganj, which was 200 miles away to the south-west. To the police it seemed that we were trying to sneak into their country through the back door. The officer had never heard of Australia, so we declared ourselves British. Time dragged on, but we eventually got the message across. We were then given some forms to fill in. I do not know what good it did because the police could not read them.

Three hours after our arrest the officer, holding out his hand, indicated that we could go. We shook hands all round then the officer said:

"Pharloot," and pointed to the distant range.

We nodded. Now, for the first time, the policemen paid attention to our packs and, after examining them, helped us on with them. The whole incident became a great joke as they demonstrated how we would look walking up the mountains with our heavy packs. After a hearty laugh, two of the men were ordered to escort us down the track for a few miles to make sure we did not get lost.

The track into the valley was extremely steep and zigzagged its way across the face of the mountain. It was good to get back into the fir forests again even though the incline was just as steep. About two o'clock, thick clouds came swirling up from the valley and within minutes we were groping through a pea soup fog like a couple of blind men. Several times we walked slap-bang into rock stupas which serve the dual purpose of marking the track as well as being Buddhist shrines.

On two occasions we, quite literally, walked on top of a party of Sherpas walking towards us, backs bent and heads lowered under the weight of their big cane baskets. We frightened hell out of the leader of the first party as we suddenly appeared from out of the blackness. In spite of his load he leapt backwards on to the second man, causing chaos along the line.

The second party had a little more warning and downed baskets to pass the time of day. Speaking in sign language, we learned that we were still on the track and that Tonelu was near.

We plodded on into the cloud with our clothes becoming wetter.

Suddenly the cloud lifted for a few seconds and we spotted a group of stone buildings ahead. Thinking this might be it, we went to investigate and managed to find a door in the biggest of the buildings before the cloud enveloped us again. It was as black as pitch inside and the door slammed shut behind us, sealing off all light. I dug my torch out of the rucksack and switched it on.

I jumped back, startled, for standing a few feet in front of me was a saffron-robed, bald headed monk, motionless and unmoved. When we recovered, we both spoke the words:

"Tonelu?"

The monk looked puzzled for a moment then broke into a chubby smile and a lot of Nepalese dialect, pointing in the direction of uphill.

Tonelu reared out of the fog and we made for the bungalow. We dumped our rucksacks on the steps and were about to look for the caretaker when two small boys popped up from nowhere and unlocked the door for us. The hut was quite large, with a kitchen, fireplace, and bunks with lumpy palliasses.

The boys brought in armloads of wood and got a fire going for us. The biggest one then dug into a cupboard and, after producing a hurricane lamp and a bottle of kerosene, proceeded to light the lamp. Before we had time to turn around they were back in again with buckets of water for us. I felt sure we were lost and had wandered into a first class hotel by mistake. Keith handed each of them some coins and they ran outside, only to return smartly with another drum of water which had to be dragged between them. I was frightened to give them any more money because I was afraid we might have the Ganges diverted to Tonelu!

Before turning in, we braved the cold night air to sit and gaze at the lights of Darjeeling twinkling in the distance and the ghostly white crown of Kangchenjunga.

I was woken next morning by a loud thumping on our door. Keith was still dead to the world so I dressed and staggered to the door. When I opened it, the two little boys burst into the room and took over lighting the fire, then darted out to fill the water buckets. I followed them out but was stopped in my tracks by a wonderful view of the snow-capped Himalayan Range with mighty Kangchenjunga, standing out from the rest with a great snow plume flying from its summit. I raced inside to wake Keith and get my camera.

After tipping the energetic bungalow guardians, we set off uphill in a beautiful crystal clear morning. The ground was covered with ice and frozen snow, and not having the proper boots, we found the going hard. The way was marked with stone stupas, which made navigation easy for us. We had company on the track, with six porters trotting along ahead of us, carrying large boxes on their backs. I do not know what was in the boxes, but they only looked heavy when the porters put them down.

Another Nepalese gentleman we met looked really colourful, with riding breeches like trousers, woven jacket and over size skullcap. He was armed with a monstrous kukri, which he grabbed every time I tried to manoeuvre into position to take a photograph of him. Unlike the rest of his people he was very unsociable towards us.

We broke from forest onto the crest of the razorback ridge, just in time to meet some fellow walkers. Coming up the ridge ahead of us were two gaily-dressed Everest-type Sherpas complete with climbing boots, ice picks, ropes and huge packs. Behind them was a tall lean Englishman also fitted out with climbing gear and several cameras. When he saw us his opening remark was,

"Hello! Where are your Sherpas?"

"We have none," Keith replied.

The Englishman blinked. "But how do you find the way?"

I dug into my pocket and pulled out a screwed up, torn piece of paper and showed him our map.

"Where do you come from?" he asked.

"Australia."

He shook his head.

"Ah – mind if I take a photo of you two?"

"No, not in the least," I answered, "go for your life."

He wished us luck and disappeared over the crest.

We were now starting the climb to Sandakphu at 12,700 feet and were plodding along over slushy ground, snow and ice. This is the highest we had been and we were feeling the effects of the altitude. At two o'clock, almost to the minute, those thick grey clouds came swirling back and visibility again dropped to feet. It was shortly after this that we passed the Sandak-Phu hut in the cloud – thanks to me. We both saw a misty shape through the cloud; Keith thought it was the hut while I insisted that it was a monastery, so we carried on.

At 13,200 foot we were met by eight porters jogging their way up through the cloud and stopped to pass the time of day with them. We spoke our current Nepalese word "SandakPhu" and all the porters excitedly pointed back the way we had come. It was too far back in the cloud so we decided to make use of our tent and camp. Now, all we had to do was to find a place to pitch it. The cloud lifted enough to allow us to find a spot down in the saddle, so we stumbled off smartly while we could still see it.

A gale sprang up, and the wind howled about us, lashing at the tent. I was forced to find big rocks to hold the tent down and then, when returning, could not find it. We had pitched just off the track (or rather a small canyon worn by Nepalese feet through the centuries) and in the fog we had to be careful not to fall into it. Sleet began to fall and it got bitterly cold. We got into our sleeping bags and made cocoa on the metho stove, then snuggled in, hoping the tent would stay with us.

We had just settled in, when we heard something outside.

"I wonder if it's a snow leopard? They're supposed to be here."

Keith said, "I'm not going out to look. It's too cold. If it comes in here, I'll give it the chop." – and at that, we went to sleep.

I woke first next morning, to find the tent frozen stiff. Wriggling myself round in my sleeping bag, I opened the tent flap and poked my nose out. The scene was like something from the Arctic, for everything was ice and snow. I put my boots on and braved the cold to view the scenic grandeur of the Himalayas in the dawn.

Keith joined me. We ignored the view and stared at the large cat paw marks in the snow, circling around the tent!

We had indeed, had a visitor!

All was quiet and we were waiting for our gear to dry out when over the hill came a happy bunch of porters talking loudly to each other. Our presence was an excuse for them to have a rest, and they lost no time in dropping their packs. We had a hilarious conversation in sign language and finally I was allowed to photograph the colourful group in their tight-legged trousers, long shirts, and odd caps.

Our next stop was Pharloot and the track dropped steeply to a beautiful fir forest ablaze with rhododendrons and other wild flowers. We came to a track junction, one led to Rimbrick and the other, to Pharloot. We decided to take the Rimbrick route as it looked more interesting.

On entering a big forest we were stopped by a man who told us he was a ranger.

"Going to Rimbrick?" he enquired.

"Yes, is this the track?"

"Yes, are you armed?" Keith showed him his Kukri while I shrugged my shoulders.

"Why?" I asked.

"There is a big forest ahead of you and we have been having trouble with the irritable Brown Bear of late. They have been attacking people passing through the forest."

"I don't feel like going back," Keith said, "will you allow us through?"

The Ranger thought for a moment.

"It's only a maybe," he answered, "but I think it will be alright. Anyway, you may be lucky enough to see a giant panda.

This is the only place outside of China where they are found."

That did it. I selected myself a waddy from a nearby wood heap and we set off, prepared to take our chances with a bear with a bad liver.

Rhododendron, magnolia, gentian and daphne were in full bloom, filling the dark green forest with colour and perfume. As we walked along the poorly defined track, we kept one eye out for the pandas and the other out for brown bears.

We arrived safely at a small Nepalese village beyond the forest and were now on a well-worn porter's track, which dropped into a 5000 feet deep gorge and to the village of Rimbrick. The grade was terribly steep and we were walking on huge smooth flagstones which the villagers had laid to help prevent erosion. Walking on these for us was murderous, as my knee and Keith's feet were now much the worse for wear.

Passing through small villages, we paused to watch women outside their houses spinning wool and pounding grain into flour with stone mallets. In the terraced garden, crops of potatoes, maize, cabbages, tomatoes and shallots grew. The plumbing and irrigation was very effective, with long lengths of bamboo lashed together to feed the water from the springs to their farms and houses. Further down, we got a wonderful view of the Rangut River soaring down, with its waterfalls and cataracts, filling the gorge with turbulence.

The track between Rimbrick and Pool Bazaar was uphill all the way, over the great rounded cobblestones. Packhorses were now being used and we saw a little less of the porters.

We arrived at Pool Bazaar very footsore and stopped at a Governmental Building to enquire about the track to Darjeeling. An English-speaking clerk informed us that we were back in India and were in a Government outpost in West Bengal. We were about to leave when we were offered a lift in a jeep to Darjeeling and so, could rest our poor legs for those twenty miles.

Pool Bazaar is one of those places where one can buy almost anything and everything, second-hand or new. I had dumped my rucksack and was going for a stroll when suddenly I saw a familiar looking Land Rover in front of me and a voice called out,

"What the hell are you chaps doing here?"

It was Captain Bajanbasi again. We told him our story and after a pause he said,

"I'll have you know you have created a bit of a record for the trip."

"Why, how come?" I asked.

"Well, for a start, no-one walks after 2 p.m. in the high country because the clouds come down and cut visibility to nil. On top of that, you were too blasted lousy to hire Sherpas. You must be crazy."

"But nobody told us about the cloud," we protested.

At this the Captain became most upset and said,

"I'll look into this matter myself when I get back to Darjeeling. Sorry I can't give you a lift up, but I have two others with me and a fair load on the old bomb now."

At this point, a jeep bounced its way into the bazaar, driven by a wild-eyed Indian. It was to take us on the long haul to Ghumm station. The Captain introduced us to the driver, then departed.

"See you in Darjeeling," he called as the "Bomb" rattled off, backfiring loudly. The jeep that we were to ride in was the local bus and carrying service from Darjeeling to Pool Bazaar, and the only means of communication between the Bazaar area and the outside world. The jeep track was only meant for foot traffic and packhorses, and in places was just barely wide enough to let the jeep through.

Of all the jeep rides I have ever had, this was be the most exciting and hair raising. The driver was an expert and did his utmost to impress us with his talent. He charged across creeks, boulders and around curves with a ferocity that nearly lost him his passengers. The road climbed 4,000 feet, most of this through tea plantations.

We were rocketing our way along a deep-channelled track when our driver suddenly hit the brakes and tried to skid the jeep to a halt.

Too late! With a glancing blow, we slewed off a parked Land Rover in the middle of the track and ploughed deep into the bank beside it. No-one was hurt; in fact everyone seemed to enjoy it. The Land Rover with which we had collided was Captain Bajanbasi's. Apparently the steering had failed again.

Both drivers treated the entire affair as a huge joke, and after having a good laugh settled down to the problem of getting the jeep past the immobile Land Rover.

With muscle power assisting the engine, and to the sound of scraping metal, the Land Rover was pushed and driven at an almost vertical angle up the wall of the channel, which was about twelve feet high at this point. The Land Rover positioned, the jeep was driven up the opposite bank at the same almost impossible angle and squeezed past.

When the jeep had regained the horizontal position in front of the Land Rover, all hands helped to get the other vehicle back on the track. The jeep passengers climbed back on board and with a wave and a shower of dirt, we said goodbye to Captain Bajanbasi.

At the end of this jeep's run, we transferred to another whose engine was completely kaput to the extent that we coasted all the way down from Ghumm to Darjeeling with only the brakes to hold us. The bomb had no hood, the doors were wired on, and by the time we reached Darjeeling, we were well and truly frozen in our cramped positions.

The following day, our reporter friend visited us in our hotel. He said the road from Darjeeling to Katmandu was not advisable, as it was really wild country. We had had intentions of visiting Sikkim and Bhutan, but found we had to be in possession of a visa twenty-one days prior to the date of entry. Since this was out of the question we reluctantly decided to move out next morning in the general direction of Katmandu, via Patna.

Washing by The Ganges

From Darjeeling, towards the Himalayas

Our wild driver, Darjeeling

CHAPTER FIVE

We passed straight through Siliguri and took the road for Malda. We were now back on the hot, dry plains amongst the flies and dust and looking forward more than ever to the cool of Katmandu.

By dusk that night we were twenty miles from Malda and began looking for a campsite. A herd of cows and buffaloes were crossing the road just in front of us, so I slowed down to allow them to cross.

Just as I twisted the throttle to pick up speed again a buffalo charged out of the ditch. He whacked the front of the scooter and sent it careering across the road. I took a header straight over the handlebars and ploughed face first into thick grey dust with Keith on top of me. The scooter was left lying on the road with the motor revving violently.

When Keith got off my back, I dug myself out of the dust, shaking myself to make sure I was all in one piece. I was covered in the fine grey dust from head to foot, while Keith was almost spotless. The only damage to the scooter was the front wheels and handlebars, which were out of alignment by about 45°.

Keith looked at me and said dryly,

"We ought to go on tour as a belly flop combination."

Spitting out dust, I effected repairs.

Next morning we reached the Ganges where we found a Mississippi style paddle-wheeler moored to the bank. Before loading we checked with the Captain to make sure we could get the scooter off the other side. He assured us we could, and on the strength of this we bought our tickets and wheeled Mirrabooka onto the old steamer.

We made ourselves comfortable in deck chairs and in a few minutes the intense glare drowsed us into a deep sleep.

We woke up smartly when we saw that our jetty was no more than a flimsy bamboo structure. Two rows of bamboo poles about two feet apart were sticking six feet out of the water, acting as pylons. More bamboo was lashed between and across them to complete this skeleton like jetty, which was about thirty feet long.

The steamer was eased against the structure, barely touching it but enough to make it creak loudly as it was pushed off plumb. We were looking at it when the Captain came down to us.

"I don't think it safe for you and machine. I will take you back for half price!"

Keith argued with him while I examined the jetty.

"I reckon we can make it, Keith."

The Captain did his best to stop us, telling us we would drown when we fell into the Ganges.

I started Mirrabooka up and eased her onto the jetty. The

bamboo creaked as it took the full weight, and the jetty gangway was just wide enough to allow us to pass along between two low rails. I straddled the machine and edged it forward and Keith walked behind me giving me directions, though I doubt if I heard half of them as the jetty was slowly sinking into the mud and I had to keep moving.

Several times I thought – 'This is IT' – as the bamboo underneath cracked and split. The scooter bounced off the last lath, onto terra firma and I gave a big sigh of relief which was short lived as an officious looking character poked out his hand and demanded 'Landing Fees'.

He never had a chance to make another move as I screwed the throttle in and left him standing in a cloud of dust. I waited for Keith to catch me up at the top of the hill about a hundred yards from the river.

According to our road directions we had a good road ahead of us, but in actual fact there were twenty miles of unmade road and for about the next ten we had to drive across dry, trackless paddy fields. If it had not been for the surveyor's pegs we probably would have got well and truly lost. At times Keith had to walk in front, shifting rocks and sods of earth to make a track for Mirrabooka, but we eventually came to the supposed road, which was nothing more than a gravel track over low rocky hills.

Now we understood why the A.A. had asked for a report.

At 2 p.m. we reached the bitumen and cruised along the open road into a hot, dry, scorching wind.

Going up a long incline, we passed a wedding procession with the bride and bridegroom being carried in separate, heavily curtained sedan chairs by profusely perspiring men who were jogging along with their loads at a fair pace ... ...

The first stop for the next day was Bhagalpur where we took on a full load of fuel and water, as there was a long dry run ahead of us to Bihar.

We were cruising along nicely when suddenly the throttle cable snapped. I pulled up in the shade of a big tree to inspect the damage, and discovered that the cable had broken inside the carburettor. As one might expect in a case like this, we were miles from anywhere, on a waterless stage, with no spare cable.

I sat beside the scooter staring at it, trying to get inspiration.

Then an idea hit me - welding wire! Before leaving Brisbane, Neil Gunn of Sear and Gunn, had given me a reel saying,

"It's wonderful stuff. You can do anything with it!"

I dug it out and tried it for size. Too thick! Not to be outdone, I got down on the road with two spanners and hammered the wire out into a long, thin strip. After some tricky work with the pliers, and a lot of patience, the cable was mended and even though I did not think so at the time, this repair job was strong enough to take us 3,500 miles before it was replaced.

*****

The run into Patna was another of those never-to-be-forgotten stretches, and it started just outside Bihar. The road was cluttered up with ox-carts and plagued by hell drivers delivering new cars from Calcutta. To make it more interesting a runaway, overcrowded passenger train rattled its way over numerous level crossings scattering ox-carts before its mad rush, and turning road traffic into chaos.

As the sun set we were plagued by millions of flying insects, which pounded us, clouding everything, for mile after mile. We had a choice of routes into Patna but, running true to form, we took the one that was to lead us through the longest bazaar in India, eight miles of screaming humanity.

The main street of the bazaar consisted of narrow, pot-holed bitumen with an equally wide stretch of dust covered ground on either side. Open-fronted bazaar shops displayed their merchandise in the dusty haze of the weak lighting.

The street had a thousand smells, a combination of curry, perfumes and foul open drains. I chugged along at a steady 15 mph, dodging people of many races, doing battle with cheeky rickshaw drivers, until my goggles became so dusted over that I had to take them off. It was not long before my eyes began to water and became sore from the dust and smoke.

I was following a big red bus and was about halfway along the street when we got caught in a traffic jam. A truck coming towards us was trying to get past a horse and sulky, the driver of which refused to move. The drivers of the bus, truck and sulky all started abusing each other and bystanders joined in, making it bedlam. Taking advantage of the discord, I edged the scooter forward around the bus and in doing so cut in on a rickshaw driver who screamed abuse at me. Keith returned the abuse in his native tongue while I concentrated on squeezing past the horse and sulky, but the noise and sight of the scooter sent the animal berserk.

Its eyes bulged as it bucked and kicked, churning up the soft dirt into a grey cloud. It was now mass confusion with bodies scattered in all directions and the horse, as it bolted, ploughed into an open-fronted shop displaying brassware and pottery.

When we eventually broke out of it, we were caked in dust and I could hardly open my eyes. By pure luck I found my way into the city square and was just heading for the Dak Bungalow when a blue Ford Consul pulled up alongside us and an English voice boomed out,

"A long way from home aren't you?"

The car stopped in front of us and we pulled up. A tall, well-built Englishman got out.

"Where are you headed?" he asked.

"The Dak Bungalow," I replied.

"How long will you be staying in Patna?"

"Two or three days."

"In that case," said the stranger, "you can come and stay with me. Follow me." He jumped into the car and, with tyres screaming and people scattering before him, tore off down a narrow side street.

My eye sight improved quickly (as I did not want to lose our Santa Claus), and I screwed the throttle in to give chase.

The car swung in an open gateway between two high stone walls. On the right wall was the British coat of arms. As we pulled up by the steps of the huge white building, the Englishman dumped out and introduced himself.

"I am Mr. Jasper, British Consul. Terribly sorry, but I am in a hurry. I have to take two guests to a cocktail party. I will just have time to show you your room and order dinner for you."

He called two boys dressed in white to carry our dusty packs to our room then beckoned us to follow him. He showed us to an enormous bedroom with adjoining bath and toilet and a balcony.

"In case you get bored, make yourself at home in the lounge. There is a cocktail bar and stereogram there, also a pile of records. I have one of the boys running a hot bath for you and dinner will be served in one hour." Apologising again for having to leave, he raced back to his car.

Keith and I retired to our room to recover and make sure that the mad bazaar had not affected us. This was too good to be true. A knock came at the door.

"Your bath is waiting, Sahib!"

We tossed a coin. I won and swaggered into the bathroom to have one of the most enjoyable baths ever. We donned our only good clothes, a nylon shirt and army trousers, and polished our boots.

The official announcement, "Dinner is served, Sahibs" was a musical sound to our starving stomachs. We dined by candlelight, being waited on at the table by a very efficient servant. Then, after dinner, we relaxed in the lounge and sipped coffee while listening to the stereogram, until Mr. Jasper and his friends returned at 11 p.m.

After breakfast next morning, Mr. Jasper asked what we had seen of Patna. "Nothing," we told him, "except the bazaar area and the Consulate.

"I will be busy this morning, but I would like you all to take my car and see the sights in comfort." He turned to the visitors from Calcutta.

"Better make sure to be back for lunch as I have to take you to the airport."

Road to Katmandu (Terraced paddy fields)

Company on a river crossing of the Ganges

'The big men were concerned about our welfare ...'

'We started on the climb to Sandakphu ...'

'We had an hilarious conversation in sign language ...'

Captain Bajanbasi behind the wheel in his battered Land Rover

'The Golden Temple ... floating on its own reflection ...'

Washing on the banks of the Ganges

A landmark of the city is a huge dome-shaped granary, built by a Captain Jon Listing in 1786 to combat famine. The enormous structure with its four feet thick walls was never filled and today stands as a memorial in the centre of a beautiful parkland. From here we drove along a broad, tree-lined avenue, featuring red flowering cotton trees, to Government House and the University. Around the city area we saw countless numbers of small doobi-donkeys pattering their way along with enormous loads on their backs and being flogged by their owners to keep them moving ... ...

After breakfast next morning, Mr. Jasper summoned his personal barber and under his supervision we were again made presentable to society. The most noticeable effect of the hair cut (to us) was that our skid-lids now fitted again.

As we were now anxious to make tracks to Nepal, Mr. Jasper looked up the ferry timetables for us. There was one due at three that afternoon. Before leaving we were told to drop in on our return from Katmandu.

"If I happen to be away," he added, "see my secretary and he will do his best for you and make you at home." ... ...

*****

A shock was waiting for us when we arrived at the ferry for this was the ordinary passenger service and was not equipped to carry anything larger than a push-bike. The vehicle ferry, which we should have caught, was a few miles further upstream and ran at noon daily. Mr. Jasper had, in his willingness to help, got his ferries a little mixed up.

Having started out we did not feel like going back. After much effort we got Mirrabooka down the long flight of concrete steps to the landing stage and arrived at the bottom short of breath and with aching arms. Before being allowed to board the ferry I was asked to empty the fuel tank as the paddle-wheeler had an open boiler.

This meant getting another tin so I raced off to make the purchase.

Ten minutes later I returned to find Keith almost submerged by the mob. I forced my way through them to find Keith most upset and on the verge of punching an over-officious Indian on the nose. Apparently the offender had been demanding to see his passport, telling Keith it was his duty to check on strangers.

My appearance caused a distraction and Keith's antagonists switched their attentions to me.

"Where are you from, and what is your position?" a leering native asked.

"Me? I am an Eskimo in charge of a weather station in the Sahara."

This gave them food for thought, and while they were discussing it I set about draining the tank before embarking on our third crossing of the Ganges.

The trip was most enjoyable and we soon made friends who offered us lots of suggestions, including one that we should eat plenty of onions to protect us from the heat. In each instance we were greeted with the same phrases,

"From where are you coming? Where is your wife? What is your work?"

We found the second question the trickiest, as their Eastern minds could not understand why two fellows our age were not married and we found ourselves being looked upon as a couple of freaks ... ...

For about twenty miles from our campsite we had a run on good bitumen, then we entered a belt of road construction and semi-bridged rivers. The detours were as usual dusty and rough, but it was the river crossing that gave us a real thrill. Two of the rivers were spanned by pontoon bridges, one of them a standard army type pontoon with the exception that it was like a switchback railway, and the other was a real beaut – it was made of log pontoons, decked with smaller logs and topped by thick bark. Riding across the bark surface was a peculiar sensation and it gave us the feeling that we were riding on sponge rubber. It was quite a battle to keep upright in places and even trickier when we came to places where the bark had been washed away by the fast flowing river, leaving a gaping hole in the decking.

As we neared the border, we were stopped twice by Nepalese police to have our passports and the scooter checked. At the second check point I accidentally handed my passport to the policeman upside down and back to front. To my surprise he checked it that way and handed it back to me, obviously not aware of the difference.

At midday, we entered the dusty, frontier town of Amlekhganj where there was a barrier across the road. We were directed by a policeman to the Customs building and were marched straight past a group of Indian and Nepalese officials and ushered into a guarded back room where we were invited to be seated. A well-dressed officer behind the desk then asked to see our passports and the carnet for the scooter.

While the documents were being stamped, he asked why we wished to visit Nepal. He was concerned with our journey to Katmandu and warned us of the rough and sometimes dangerous ten-hour run ahead of us.

"That's the average time taken by the big trucks on the 185 mile road, which is only thirty two miles in a straight line," he said. With a final warning about fuel and water, we were allowed to go. We changed our money at a money-changer's room behind a produce shop, then set off out of town, pursued by dozens of cheeky, ragged children.

At the end of the first horror stretch we passed through some small villages and then wound our way among low, heavily forested hills.

We were slugging away up a steep hill when we were flagged down by an Englishman driving a Land Rover.

"I say, where are you two off to?" he said.

"Katmandu!"

He shook his head.

"You'll never make it on that machine, you have to make a deep river crossing ahead and apart from that the road is falling to pieces. Look out for the big trucks that career down the mountain. They are driven by Sikhs, and they are a wild lot."

As though we did not know.

With these happy thoughts in mind we thanked him and moved on. Half an hour later we came to an extremely steep hill which had a tunnel cut through for the up traffic and the road over the top for the down traffic. This was the Churia Tunnel, two hundred yards long, dark, wet and greasy with moss and seepage. We skated our way through. The road followed up a valley for some miles till we came to the river crossing, which had been bridged – at least until the monsoon flood had partly washed the bridge away. The only way across was a ford, about forty yards wide and a good four feet deep, with the river running fast.

Since it was impossible to get the scooter across the ford, we decided to inspect the bridge.

It was not quite as bad as it looked. There was a six feet piece missing out of the middle and half of the original planking was still intact. We decided to rebuild it enough to get the scooter across. After shifting a few sleepers around and moving some rubble, all was ready. I started the scooter and rode it on to the shaky construction, which was about thirty feet above the river.

The trickiest part was the drive across the foot-wide plank spanning the six feet wide gap. I gave a sigh of relief when I parked the scooter an the opposite bank and waited for Keith to catch me up.

"We made it!" I thought, "but we'll still have to cross it on the return trip."

The road wound amongst rugged hills and crossed dry riverbeds until we reached the village of Bhaisa at 1,500 feet at the base of the big climb. Away in the mountains a big storm was brewing with an ominous black sky and much lightning.

After a passport examination, the village police sergeant took pity on us and found us shelter in a bamboo hut while the scooter was garaged under the police station for the night. We had just climbed into our sleeping bags when we heard a noise under the platform on which we were sleeping.

I grabbed the torch while Keith made a dive for the machette. Shining the torch down, I was surprised to see a small, petrified boy crouching against the wall. When I spoke to him he bolted like a frightened animal out through a hole in the laths. When all was quiet again he returned and this time we saw what he was after. We had taken his bed for the night, and now he curled up on a bench and wrapped himself in torn blankets, prepared to take his chances with us in preference to the cold outside.

We rose early next morning, then set off towards the formidable looking mountain range.

The road followed up a deep gorge, winding up steep grades and over huge wash-aways. Soft white sand heaped up on the curves made it hard work for the scooter and us. We paused at the 4,000 feet mark to admire the views and the huge rhododendron trees ablaze with colour standing out against the other moss and orchid festooned trees.

From the Simbhanjang Pass at 8,126 feet, the road rose and fell as we wound our way through the Himalayan foothills into a completely new world. The soil was a deep, rich red colour and wherever possible the steep slopes were terraced with deep green paddy fields, making a patterned contrast to the Himalayan backdrop.

Scattered about the deep valleys were dozens of small villages bringing life to the scene. Road construction gangs were busily repairing damage done by the previous monsoon season, with groups of workers sitting by huge piles of rocks breaking them up with little hammers. Time seemed no object to these men. Whenever we passed through a village we were attacked by packs of children. We eventually corkscrewed our way up a bitumen stretch to a 5,000 feet pass, the entrance to the magnificent

Katmandu valley.

Before us lay the broad, lush, saucer-like valley with the high mountains sweeping up on all sides. Terraced paddy fields cut their striking and distinctive pattern into the valley slopes.

Eight miles from Katmandu we passed through the 3000 year-old city of Paten, an ancient capital of Nepal. From here on we ran a gauntlet of police road blocks and for the first time since South India I found it necessary to drive with my thumb on the horn as people wandered aimlessly across the road.

Mr. Jasper had given us a letter of introduction to Mr. Clough of the British Council in Katmandu, suggesting that Mr. Clough might be able to assist us in some way.

Our hotel was a three-storied, red brick place run by a Bengali well known to Mr. Clough. Because of this, we were given the best room in the building. To get to it we followed a rabbit warren-like passageway to a flight of narrow, rickety wooden steps to the top floor – taking care not to bump our heads on the six feet high ceilings. At the end of another collapsing corridor was our room. It was twelve feet square with a six feet six inches high ceiling and an earth floor laid over six-inch planking with two coir mats by two ancient beds ... ...

*****

As an expedition into the higher foothills was out of the

question, Mr. Clough offered to lend us his Land Rover to see as much as possible. It was arranged for us to have a day on foot and the rest of our time in the Land Rover in the company of a guide.

Of all the museums I have ever visited, the one in Katmandu (which was once part of the palace) must have the greatest collection of knives and swords I have ever seen – a sign of the National pastime.

To reach the stupa of Bodhnath, which is situated on a high hill, it was necessary to climb four hundred stone steps. We were joined by a party of pilgrims and progress was slow for they stopped regularly at prayer stations. On entering the courtyard at the top, an enormous five feet high bell was rung by the Buddhists to let Buddha know they had arrived. Smaller prayer bells and prayer wheels lined the base of the high domed stupa, on the top of which stood the magnificent four-sided gold leaf tower topped by a conical spire. This is one of the most beautiful pieces of work in Katmandu, with the former bearing four pairs of weird blue eyes, one on each side to watch over the city. Overhead, hundreds of colourful prayer flags attached to ropes flutter in the breeze.

While I was busy taking photos, Keith was approached by a Tibetan refugee dressed in woollen knee-boots, a long red and green tunic, and a bowler hat. He was selling Tibetan coins and found Keith a ready buyer.

After dinner that evening, we stumbled our way up the dark stairway of our hotel and fumbled our way along a pitch-black hall to our door. When I finally located the keyhole and entered the room, I discovered that our light bulb had been taken out. With the aid of the dim street light, I located a torch and stumbled my way back down the stairs to the manager.

"The light bulb in our room is missing. Could I have another one please?"

"But you had one last night, don't you know we have to share them?" he protested, most upset.

However, after a little persuading I managed to get one out of him and returned to our room feeling as though I had robbed the place.

After breakfast next morning, we made for the Residency. Mr. Clough introduced us to his Number One man, and gave him instructions not to scratch his new Land Rover when he took us on our tour.

Katmandu has something like 300 temples and it was now we were thankful for our guide, as he picked the best of them, showing us elaborate woodcarvings on the temples and pagodas. One of the finest buildings we saw on the day was a beautiful five-tiered pagoda, the only one outside Burma.

"This is the headquarters of the Chini Lama," said our guide as he parked the Land Rover outside an arched gate.

"If you don't mind, I'll leave you to wander around on your own. I wish to see some friends close by."

"Okay," said Keith, "we'll see you later."

In a large courtyard, groups of Tibetan refugees were wandering aimlessly around. As we finished exploring the huge dome shaped stupa, a monk approached us and beckoned us to follow him. On the way to the cluster of brick and timber buildings we were joined by three Americans and two Swedes, who had flown into Katmandu that day for a quick visit. Said one of the Americans –

"We don't know where you guys are going but we're coming too!"

So the seven of us followed the little monk into a building and up a flight of tiny rickety steps leading to the top floor. On opening the door we stood speechless. The room, about twenty feet by fifteen, was lined with thick carpets and tapestry.

Along one wall was an immense bookcase displaying everything from encyclopaedias to novels. At the far end of the room a bald bespectacled monk sat cross legged on a pile of cushions. This was the Chini Lama.

As we approached, he greeted the Americans, Keith and me in

English, and the Swedes in Swedish, and also picked Keith and me for Australians. He proceeded to give us a short lecture on Buddhism and at the same time showed us round his 'humble quarters', as he put it.

The drapes and ornaments must have been worth a fortune. I noticed a brand new stereogram in one corner of the room and nudged one of the Americans. The monk saw me.

"Surprised?" he said.

"Well, I didn't expect to see a stereogram up here," I said.

"No doubt you have one in Australia, so why shouldn't I have one here," was the reply. Not wishing to get involved in an argument, I smiled at him and moved on. General conversation broke out as the Lama told us more about Buddhism and the Tibetans who had fled from their country before the Chinese advance. His bright personality and ability to speak ten languages kept us entertained and astounded.

Mr. Clough had suggested we visit Naqarkot, a high vantage point north of Katmandu.

"In the clear early mornings," he said, "it is possible to see 270 miles of the main Himalayan Range with all its peaks, including Everest."

We loaded what gear we wanted onto the scooter and set off.

The road climbed up three thousand feet amongst rice-terraced hills and was extremely dangerous in places due to landslides. At the pass from where we had to continue the climb on foot, I bargained with one of the villagers to allow us to store the scooter until our return.

We were about to put on our rucksacks, when we were swooped on by a party of porters wanting to carry our rucksacks for us. At first we said no, but they looked so upset we could not refuse, even though it was only a three-mile walk. One of them nominated himself as guide and then selected two grinning porters to do the carrying. The price was simple, a rupee each for the carriers and two for the guide.

The guide set off at a blistering pace, leaving the two porters way behind. After about a mile Keith and I stopped to see where our porters had got to. They eventually came into view, but something was missing off their backs, our rucksacks. Our first thoughts were that they had jettisoned their loads, then suddenly we spotted our packs bobbing up and down on the track behind the strolling porters. They were being carried by two very small, heavily sweating women, who were running along behind, trying hard to keep up with their masters. Not only had the porters brought their wives but their entire families, for instead of having our expected three porters we now had a safari of fourteen.

It was uphill all the way and the track was one, so well-used that it had been worn to a depth of twenty-five feet in places.

We reached the summit in time to see the last of the sun's rays lighting up the heavily clouded Himalayan Range. The biggest surprise was to find the remains of a small, nine-hole golf course on the summit, once the world's highest golf course. We made camp beside a bunker on the edge of a tremendous gorge, on the other side of which was the 23,299 feet Mt. Ganesh Himal. Our porters lit a fire for us and warmed themselves before retreating back to the village for the night.

Next, a Nepalese gentleman appeared from out of the black night to warn us that it was not safe to camp because leopards were bad, but we said we would chance the cats and wait for the view next morning. We stoked up the fire and made a final brew which we drank by the glowing coals. It was such a beautiful night that we were reluctant to turn in, but a cold wind sprang up from the north, and, forgetting about leopards and the wonder of the Himalayas alike, we took refuge in our sleeping bags.

At first light we bounced out of our sleeping bags to view the sunrise on 270 miles of the Himalayan Range. What an anti-climax! Almost the entire Range was sheltered under a high, black cloud layer. But at least we could still see all the major peaks, including the ice-cream cone of Mt. Everest, way off in the distance, and gradually the sun filtered through giving a little more colour to the scene.

It was an unforgettable sight.

I had just made some tea to wash our breakfast down when over the hill came a party of porters followed by a heavily panting white man and woman. Our white visitors were from the German Embassy in Delhi, and had flown to Katmandu and hired the porters to bring them to this spot to view the Himalayas before returning to Germany. As they sat down beside us to recover, I served them with tea and biscuits while Keith explained how we came to be here. At this point, the sky began to break a little more and looking westward we could see Dhaulagiri, Annapurna, Manaslu and, to the east, Gosainthan and Cho Oyu with Mt. Everest on the extreme right.

Photos taken, our German friends departed, leaving us with an invitation to visit them so they could return the hospitality ... ...

*****

The porters and their wives had arrived to carry the packs back. It was not until we were half way down the mountains that we realised that the men had each brought along an extra wife to carry the packs.

When we reached the bottom, the guide demanded payment for himself, his two assistants and the women who carried the loads, both last night and this morning. The price had now risen to ten rupees against the three we had originally bargained for. The entire village turned out to see justice done and shouted at us to pay up as they surrounded the packs. While Keith was arguing with them I managed to wangle the guide to one side and flap two rupees in his face.

This did the trick! He was now on our side and, tucking the money away in his shirt, he turned to abuse the villagers on our behalf. At the first opportunity we darted in to capture our packs.

Leaving Keith to guard them, I went to get the scooter out of hock and was followed by a band of troublemakers, obviously coming along to see what they could stir up.

As soon as we came to the place where the scooter was garaged, the troublemakers demonstrated, telling the owner to raise the price.

I had to think of something quickly or else have the scooter held for ransom. ... In sign language I promised the owner a ride on the scooter if he got it out. This appealed to him very much and after abusing the opposition he opened the heavy wooden door. The crowd was most upset that they had lost but even more so when I took the owner for a ride on Mirrabooka. With my giggling pillion passenger jumping around behind me, I drove back to Keith.

The pillion man jumped off and did a little dance as he told the villagers about his ride, waving his arms about and making motor noises. The antics and description were very realistic and now everybody wanted a ride. The stage was set for a quick exit and as soon as Keith was on I started the motor and gradually crept through the ranks until we were clear, leaving a bunch of confused villagers in a cloud of dust ... ...

With the exception of a skid when we almost went over a 3,000 feet drop, the return trip was quiet. I even managed to get Mirrabooka over the broken bridge without too much difficulty and we arrived at Amlekhganj in one piece.

Gate Entrance to Katmandu

CHAPTER SIX

In no time we were back on the plains amongst the heat, dust and flies.

We reached the Ganges to find that we had again missed the vehicle ferry but had the choice of three passenger ferries. We managed to squeeze onto the bow of one of the paddle wheelers which was already overloaded. The skipper had to use what landing stages were available. Bamboo being rafted downstream prevented the ferry reaching the landing stage and forced the passengers to clamber over the side and stumble their way across the slippery bamboo. It cost us another five rupees to get Mirrabooka carried ashore by local workers. After an anxious five minutes, Mirrabooka was planted safely on terra firma and we rode off to the Consulate.

We were met by Mr. Jasper's secretary, who told us that Mr. Jasper was away on tour for a week, but our room was awaiting us. It was like coming home again, but this time we had the place entirely to ourselves. The secretary apologised for the cook who was not available, as he had been given the week off but he was expected to come back, in the event of guests arriving.

"I will try and locate him as soon as possible," said the secretary.

"Meanwhile help yourselves in the kitchen."

It was a hot, windy day outside and we were glad to get into the bath and soak off the dust of Nepal.

The number two servant turned up later in the evening and was appointed to prepare dinner for us. On the stroke of eight the thin little man in a khaki uniform appeared at the lounge door and mumbled something to us, at the same time pointing to the dining room. It seemed as though the boy had been given instructions and he was doing his best to carry them out. The table had been laid with an oversized white tablecloth and was cluttered up with the best of the Residences silver and china. Tucking the tablecloth around our legs we waited expectantly for our dinner.

The boy entered carrying a large silver tray and, balancing it in one hand, served out our feast. We each got a skinny cutlet, a baked potato and six chappatis. For dessert we were given a bunch of bananas. Not wishing to offend the boy who was nervously peering at us from behind the screen, we acted as though it was the best meal ever. In spite of this, we managed to offend him when we asked for some marmalade to put on the chappatis.

After breakfast of over-salted porridge next morning, I took Keith to the hospital to have his plaster removed. The secretary had kindly made arrangements for the visit, thus saving Keith a long wait. But even so he was unable to return to the Consulate till late ... ...

With Keith sporting a pale, hairless left arm we bade farewell to Mr. Jasper's secretary and handed him a note to pass on to Mr. Jasper.

We arrived at Sasaram at mid afternoon and paused to visit the enormous tomb of Sher Shar who died in 1845. The mausoleum fascinated us, mainly because it was the first large sample of Muslim architecture we had seen.

It was dark when we sighted the light of Benares (Varanasi) and, feeling particularly filthy after playing tag with fifty new cars en route to Delhi, we made straight for the Dak Bungalow. The Bungalow, which had been recommended to us, turned out to be a derelict old building that must have once been the pride of Benares.

It was a hot, sunny dusty morning when we entered this ancient, religious city on the banks of the Ganges. I was really looking forward to visiting Benares.

Riding through the crowded, winding streets, it was interesting to note the number of people wearing a red chequered handkerchief or Dhoti on their shoulders, the sign that they are natives of Benares.

Almost every shop seemed to be a market place for Pan, the betel nut leaf, which is chewed by every other person in the city.

Getting through the mob was almost impossible – riding over large smooth cobblestones and pushing our way through people, rickshaws and white cows.

"The best way to see Benares," we were told, "is to hire a boat and view the ghats from the river."

We found ourselves a seaworthy craft then bargained with the boatman for a price. We settled for two rupees with an extra one as a bonus if we got a good trip. The boatman made us comfortable on large cushions under a canvas awning and told us not to move around because the boat might capsize. A bent, old man on the stern got busy with a paddle and we were away.

We were taken downstream first, to the Assi Ghat at the southernmost end of the city where the Assi River enters the Ganges. We worked our way back slowly, keeping close to the bank and passing the Tulsi Ghat, the dwelling place of one of the Hindu poets and the scene of an annual festival. Next came the palace of Maharaja Ghait Singh whose great stone walls rise vertically from the water's edge. We passed the burning Ghat of Harishchandra then the Dasasvamedha Ghat, one of the most elaborate in Benares. This ghat is especially thronged during eclipses and is also the place where Brahma made his "ten horses sacrifice". At one end of the ghat is the low, whitewashed shrine of "Sitala", the Goddess of Smallpox.

Manikarnika Ghat, which is the most sacred of the Burning Ghats in Benares, was in use as we moved past. Three bodies were in the process of being burnt and a fourth was being prepared for cremation by three men piling wood onto the shrouded body. Close by are the towers from which the ashes are scattered into the sacred Ganges. Panchganga Ghat is a bathing ghat where people came to bath and collect urnfulls of the holy water, some of which is carried up the steps and sold to the people unable to get down to the river.

The boatman ordered the craft to be swung around but the profusely perspiring oarsman objected and went on strike.

The upset boatman, mumbling abuse at the old man, took the paddle and pulled the boat into the Mir Ghat, which is used by Muslims. We followed the boatman up the steps to the Dharm Kup, a sacred well. Nearby is a Nepalese Temple with a pagoda-style roof which is picturesque, but disfigured by carving indecent to Western eyes. The boatman led on, taking us along a maze of narrow alleys and tunnels before returning to the boat via the steep steps.

By the time we had returned to the wharf we felt we had been given our money's worth. Benares is a place where one could spend much time as its history dates back to 200 BC and is crammed full of interest. I was hoping to have witnessed one of the festivals but unfortunately we were there at the wrong time of the year.

We rode around the city trying to find a Hindu Temple that we could visit, but at this time of the year they were all closed to unbelievers. Two of the temples however, still stand out in my mind. One is the Durga, or monkey temple, surrounded by a high wall behind which the sacred monkeys live, and the other is the Siva temple with its shiny gilded pinnacles ... ...

*****

Five miles from Benares, we passed through Sarnath, the "Deer Park" and the place where Buddha preached his first sermon 2,500 years ago and set in motion the first of the Buddhists Wheels – the Wheel of Law.

It was good to get on the open road again away from the rickshaws and oxen. Out past Saranath we passed several rickshaws carrying bodies wrapped in white cloth on their way to the burning ghats.

We approached Lucknow over the flat, parched, central plain and for most of the way passed great trains of enormous long-legged camels that towered over us. We were passing a train of about thirty beasts and were halfway along the line when one of the ungainly, splay-footed creatures did a smart left hand turn right in front of us. We were doing a good thirty mph and had little hope of stopping. I was all set for a head-on collision when it spotted us and propped. I shot past underneath the arched neck, all but rubbing our noses with the camel's kneecaps. Once clear, I glanced in the rear vision mirror to see pandemonium break loose in the ranks as the frightened camels stampeded.

Lucknow, the old Muslim capital, grew out of the plains, clean and stately of outline, crowned with domes of burnished gold and minarets on its palaces, and tombs set in fine parklands. With the tall onion shaped mosques to guide us, we made for the Muslim Quarter. This was our true introduction to the Muslim world and a change from the Hindu and Buddhist ways of life.

The Turkish Gate with its Moorish architecture held our attention for some time before we moved on to visit the Asafi Mosque.

This is a magnificent building with four tall, beautiful minarets, one at each corner, towering above the gold spired dome of the mosque. We had put on canvas over-shoes when a guide attached himself to us and offered to show us around - for a fee. The main hall inside the mosque was enormous with hundreds of huge crystal chandeliers hanging from the lofty ceiling. After seeing so many Hindu and Buddhist temples with their ornate decorations we found this, our first large mosque with its clean symmetrical lines most refreshing. The guide, of whom we had taken no notice until now, volunteered to show us the maze of passageway and tunnels which were built as escape routes. We were taken up and down long flights of narrow steps, around balconies and through a most confusing labyrinth which eventually brought us out onto the roof. From here we got a wonderful view of Lucknow and of the four minarets and, later on the way back, the guide took much pride in demonstrating the whispering gallery.

We paid our guide and set out for the Shar Nagaf Palace, which must have been a gem in its heyday. Of all the beauty of the glorious parkland, only a skeleton remains ... ...

*****

Cawnpore is almost the complete opposite to Lucknow. There are no mosques dominating the skyline, just great black chimneys belching black smoke from the city's firearms industry and the cotton and jute mills. We had visited a memorial to the Indian Mutiny and were about to go shopping when we were stopped by a smartly dressed businessman.

"From Australia? Are you cricketers?" he asked.

"No," we replied.

"Oh, never mind. Come with me for refreshments," he said,

looking most disappointed. He led us into a prosperous jeweller's shop and asked us to make ourselves comfortable. Tea and sandwiches were served.

"Is there anything you are wanting from the shops?" the jeweller enquired.

"Well – we were about to buy some food and methylated spirits for cooking before you invited us in," Keith said.

Before we had a chance to say another word, two of the juniors were promptly dispatched to the market place to do our shopping for us. We wanted to go with them but our host insisted that we stay.

"They will buy for you at the right price," he assured us.

The boys returned, loaded with double quantities of everything. This was all very nice, but we now had the problem of where to put it all. With the aid of the boys we turned the motor scooter into a pack mule.

"Will you stay with us for a few days?" asked the jeweller.

"Thanks, we would love to, but we would like to get as close to Agra as we could, to be sure of being there to see the Taj Mahal by full moon tomorrow night."

"Yes, you must not miss the most beautiful sight in the world," said the jeweller, "I will forgive you and allow you to go."

We camped under the stars and awoke at daybreak next

morning to the chirping of hundreds of colourful birds that flew amongst the trees growing by the lagoon.

The morning's ride was both interesting and entertaining, passing old fortified villages, some with forty feet high walls, and also Noah's Ark – stretches of road where camels, elephants, monkeys, bears (on leashes), cranes and other bird life were in profusion.

It was mid afternoon when we drove into Agra under a heavily clouded sky.

We were trying to find a hostel, the address of which we had been given when we were rescued from a curious crowd by a Christian Indian, whom I shall call Mr. Smith (because I have forgotten his name). Mr. Smith did not know of the place we were looking for and suggested we stay at his house for a few days – if we did not mind sleeping in the open.

With his ten-year old daughter clinging to the carrier of the bicycle, Mr. Smith pedalled off through the heavy traffic at a reckless speed, darting through openings that I dare not tackle. We passed through an area that had little or no sanitation, then turned off into a narrow alleyway which led into a large clearing. At the end of the clearing was Mr. Smith's house, surrounded by a nine feet high wall.

"Leave your scooter here and come with me and meet my

family," Mr. Smith said.

He had a wife and three children and told us he had been forced to build the adobe wall to stop his Hindu neighbours from raiding the place at night.

"You can sleep on those stretchers near the tree – park your scooter beside you if you like – and bring your packs inside."

"We won't be putting you to any trouble?" we asked.

"Of course not! It will give me a chance to practise my English."

When the moon was high, we rode off through the crowded streets passing on the way a wedding procession preceded by a discordant, clashing brass band.

We bought an admission ticket then joined the crowd waiting by the Taj Mahal gate. A small door within the gate was opened and we followed the crowd into the courtyard. There it was, the Taj Mahal by full moon. An unforgettable and overpowering sight as the white marble glowed in the moonlight. We moved slowly forward past the pool to the steps of this most perfect gem of Muslim architecture, which took twenty-two years to build. We donned canvas overshoes then joined a party on a tour of inspection.

Using a hurricane lamp, our guide showed us the beautiful semi-precious stone inlay, much of which was in the form of the lotus flower. The turbaned guide demonstrated the acoustics under the high dome; standing dead centre, he lifted his head and gave a sharp call. The echo from the dome rang through the vault for a full fifteen seconds before fading out.

We followed him down a flight of steps to the vault where the Shah and his wife are entombed. Even in this smaller vault echoes lasted for a full five seconds. We were busy examining the marble and inlay when we were told it was time to leave. Time had gone all too quickly, so taking a final look at the spectacle we departed.

I do not know whether it was a blinding effect from the Taj Mahal or not, but I got horribly lost on the way home and if it had not been for a taxi driver, we may have still been there.

Next morning we were away to an early start and set off to Sikandra, five miles from Agra, and the mausoleum of Akbar. This is a beautiful building of red sandstone with marble inlay and four tall minarets of marble. The mausoleum and gardens take up an area of 150 acres and at their prime must have been wonderful. We reluctantly left and rode to the Fort of Akbar whose imposing, seventy feet high, red sandstone walls circle for a mile and a half to enclose the fort.

Parking Mirrabooka, we crossed the causeway that had been built over the moat, then passed between the enormous gates.

Inside was a small town with roads and pathways winding amongst the old buildings. We climbed up on to the walls to get a better view and walked along the broad parapet. The most elegant building in the fort is the "Pearl Mosque", with an exterior of red sandstone and an interior of marble, white, blue and grey veined.

As the sun was high in the sky, we made a daylight visit to the Taj Mahal but found things very different. The place was full of tourists darting around taking photos and getting in each other's way. We made the rounds again, then fought our way, past souvenir sellers at the entrance, to Mirrabooka.

We drove around the old quarter until we found a parking spot and then wandered along the crowded streets studying the sights which included a long-haired Jain monk clad in his birthday suit – it being against their religion to wear clothes.

*****

Crossing the vast plain on our way to Delhi we had our eardrums constantly shattered by the pop-pop-popping noise of home made, grain threshing machines. For us these machines became a feature of north-western India as every other town and village had at least one of these machines blowing smoke rings.

It was a beautiful day and we were twenty miles from Delhi when I heard a flop, flop, flop from the rear wheel – flat tyre. A nearby cycle repair shop gave me no hope of getting the tyre repaired, and as our spare was also useless I had no option but to find a vulcanising workshop.

I eventually returned with the patched tyre to find my mate in the company of a Sikh. The Sikh considered I needed a rest and took over the job of replacing the tyre.

"Now where is it you wish to go?" he enquired.

"The Youth Hostel Headquarters in Delhi," replied Keith.

"Ah, I know where that is, follow me," and with that he started up his own scooter and drove off.

Unfortunately for us, New Delhi is one of those cities laid out in circles, and by the time we reached the youth hostel headquarters, I was most confused. The "YHA HQ India was housed in a two-storied building and when our Sikh friend had seen us safely inside, he departed, wishing us luck.

In a dingy office that was littered with books and papers we were received by one of the staff.

"The hostel in the city is full, but there is another at Aroka, ten miles from here," the officer said. "It isn't as good as our city hostel. I will give you directions how to get there."

With Keith navigating from the pillion, we set off.

Aroka turned out to be in the quarter of old Delhi near Qatb Minar – the surviving 238 feet, five-storied, sandstone tower which was once the centre of the thirteenth century capital. It is now an area of vast ruins and rubble, with only a few buildings around the Qatb Minar tower left standing.

We came to a high stone wall set well back off the bitumen and if our directions were right, our hostel was behind it. We drove through a narrow gate and entered a large, sun-baked courtyard, at opposite ends of which were buildings. We looked at the two buildings and decided that one was a Buddhist monastery and the other the hostel. Mirrabooka was parked under a shady tree away from the scorching sun then, literally pushing our way through the flies, we made for the monastery where we were met by a saffron robed monk who greeted us in English.

"And where are you two boys from?"

"Australia," I replied.

"Welcome, I think you are the first Australians we have had here. You have company in the hostel. There is an American, a Swede and a German staying with us at present. Come, I will show you around."

The building consisted of a kitchen and dining room combined, a dormitory and a spare room.

"This," said the monk, "is where you hang your washing as nothing is safe outside."

"Where do we get our water?" I enquired.

"There is a well behind the monastery. Be careful, it is deep."

We unloaded Mirrabooka, then claimed two of the bunks in the dormitory. Being overdue for a bath, we armed ourselves with buckets and soap, dirty clothes and set off to the well.

After a little practice we managed to fill the buckets, then we took our bath in the open air.

"Better boil this water," Keith said, "Look at the animal life in it."

Keith was making tea on the metho stove when the door opened and in walked a short, stocky character. He had the biggest black handlebar moustache I have ever seen and was dressed in a huge battered straw hat, swim trunks, thongs and was carrying a bucket.

"Hello," I said, unable to take my eyes off the moustache and feeling as though I should address him as 'Pedro'.

"You are the Australians," he said.

We introduced ourselves, but he insisted we call him Swede.

His travelling companion, the American, arrived shortly afterwards and we all sat and talked over a cup of tea. The two boys had arrived the day before after travelling across Europe, then North Africa via Libya, Egypt, Sudan and Kenya, where they got mixed up with the Mau Mau terrorists. From Kenya, they had taken a tramp steamer across the Indian Ocean to Bombay and then a train to Delhi. Just on dusk we were joined by another wanderer, a German, who had just returned from Kashmir. Apart from our metho stove the only other cooking device was a primus, so we had to cook tea in relays.

Next morning the other boys were suffering badly from dysentery and Keith and I were only just in better condition. We were the only ones who had any pills, which fortunately brought some relief to the suffering. We donned our freshly washed clothes then, after a wander around the city, went in search of the Persian Embassy. We found it tucked away in one of the diplomatic quarters and on entering the building were met by a stocky Persian who gave us a pile of forms to fill in. The forms were taken, then half an hour later we were called into a room where we were interviewed by a sharp-featured little man.

"Why do you want to go to Persia," he asked.

We gave him a great list of reasons, then he set about preparing our visas which cost us 2/- compared with one pound each for the others.

"Any questions?" he asked.

"Yes," I said and started to rattle off a list, but was not allowed to finish for the Persian cut in with,

"Why not? You pay your rupee, you do what you will."

I pondered over this reply, wondering what the catch was.

We completed our diplomatic calls then turned tourist and visited the famous Red Fort.

The red sandstone fort with its maze of arcades and galleries reminded us very much of the Agra Fort. The great courtyards are now represented by lawns and shrubberies which are maintained by the government and at the time of our visit were a picture. Of the buildings that are left intact within the fort, possibly the most beautiful is the Pietra Dura Room which was once used to house the invaluable Peacock Throne during its sojourn in India ... ...

*****

Two days later a most depressed East German chap arrived at the hostel and it was some hours before we found out why he was so upset. Apparently, some months previously he had escaped from East Germany and had hitched as far as Tehran where he was robbed of all he had. After working for some time there, he saved enough money to move on to India. He had left some of his gear at Aroka while he visited Kashmir, only to return today to find that what gear he had left behind had been stolen and now all he had left was a few ragged clothes. We all did what we could to comfort him and chipped in what we could to keep him going for a few days until he could reach his Embassy.

I spent the next morning servicing Mirrabooka and on riding back to Aroka found the American boy very sick with dysentery. He had about reached the end of his tether and in desperation decided to go and see if the monk would help him. He was away for almost two hours, but came back smiling and told us that the monk had given him a mixture to take and he now felt a lot better.

"That monk is 'real Mickey Mouse'," he said.

I was not sure what this expression implied so we asked him.

"Mickey Mouse. Well that means the guy has really been around and has visited the States and Disneyland."

"Oh," I said, feeling much enlightened, having never heard of a Buddhist Monk being 'Mickey Mouse' before.

In the evening the Swede and I took a trip into the market place on Mirrabooka to do the shopping and had just finished when we were attracted by a large crowd. In the centre of the throng, sitting crossed-legged on a mat, was a Hindu Holy man with long black hair and beard. He seemed to be in a trance and was muttering quietly when he picked up a broad-bladed knife and slashed himself across the thighs, making his legs bleed. The trance deepened, and after a few minutes the bleeding gradually stopped. The Swede and I were held fascinated but were soon returned to reality by a stirring crowd. We took the hint and left quickly, feeling perplexed as we rode back to Aroka.

Exploring the Qatb Minar was fun; the climb up the spiral staircase left us with leg muscles like rocks, but the 360 degree view was worth it. Close by the tower is one of the most curious antiquities in India. Standing in an ancient temple courtyard surrounded by carved stone pillars is a solid shaft of wrought iron 23 feet 8 inches high and 16 inches in diameter, dating back to the eleventh century ... ...

We checked out with the Australian High Commission and headed for the Punjab, the land of the Sikhs. We were hardly over the border when we noticed a big change in the country. The normally dry, parched land was thriving, with green crops of many kinds and the country, as far as the eye could see, was under irrigation. We passed through the towns of Panipat, Karnal and Ambala and the turbaned, bearded Sikhs became a common sight. Even the towns themselves looked cleaner.

Amritsar, present capital of the Punjab and the old depot for the central Asian markets, is another of India's intriguing cities. We crawled through the congestion of the narrow streets and alleyways with my thumb pressed hard on the horn until I was unable to move either way - blocked by almost an impenetrable wall of humanity. We might have known that we would not be stranded for long in the capital of the Punjab. Suddenly, a tall, young Sikh came to our rescue, squeezing his way through the crowd.

"Where is it you wish to go?" he called out.

"Anywhere, as long as we can get out of this crowd," I answered.

"Stay close to me and I will try and get you out."

With the motor revving I sneaked Mirrabooka forward behind our shouting rescuer.

After what seemed ages we broke out into a large square, something I did not think existed in this part of the world.

"My name is Surinder Singh. I am a draughtsman. I work in the town hall," he said breathing heavily.

"Where are we?" I asked.

"In the square which fronts the Golden Temple and the Sikh Hostel," he said, pointing them out.

"Would you like to come with me and have dinner with my family? You could leave your scooter in the Hostel. It would be safe there."

Keith and I glanced at each other, then said, "Yes."

We followed Surinder back along the narrow chasm-like streets and into four feet wide alleyways, until we came to a door.

"Up here," Surinder said, and we followed him up a long flight of steps on to the fourth floor. We stepped into a neatly-furnished room and were introduced to the family, then asked to sit at a low table. When we had eaten Surinder said,

"There is a festival on at the Golden Temple and I have to go there now. Would you like to come along with me? It's something you should see. Non-Sikhs are not usually allowed into the Temple at this time, but I think you two ought to pass for Sikhs with your beards and tanned skins."

We returned to the crowded streets, pushing our way past open-fronted bazaars where turbaned men sat smoking their hookahs between sales.

Underneath the clock tower by the Temple's entrance Surinder told us to remove our boots and socks and check them into the 'cloakroom' – making sure we got a receipt. This done we were taken to a long marble trough where we washed our feet.

"Take your handkerchief and cover your head and stay close to me and do exactly as I do."

The Golden Temple, standing in the centre of a large tank, looked as though it was floating on its own reflection. The temple and its surroundings were lit by hundreds of coloured lights and the copper gilt of the temple seemed to glow. Hundreds of pilgrims with feet still wet from the trough, walked over the tessellated, black and white marble pavement, wetting it so that it reflected the Temple image on the marble.

We walked around the edge of the eighteen feet deep tank to a narrow, brilliantly lit causeway which led out to the Temple. At the gate Keith and I were searched to make sure we had no cameras with us and in the company of Surinder were allowed to go through. When we reached the Temple entrance, Surinder told us to be extremely careful and not walk on the marble slab which lay across the threshold.

"It is sacred," he said, "and has to be kissed by Sikhs as they enter so don't put your foot on it."

Surinder kneeled down and kissed it while Keith and I cautiously stepped over.

We were now in a long queue that filed round the Temple. We had not gone far when we were given holy water to drink and a garland of flowers to wear. Entering the main hall we were then given a handful of sweetmeats which only after much difficulty I was able to swallow. The big hall was crowded and in the centre, sat the high priest with the 'Granth' or holy book before him. Nearby was a sheet spread out over the floor and pilgrims were throwing offerings onto it. Turbaned men were beating drums and playing flutes and string instruments, while the pilgrims chanted verses from the Granth. The air was full of the pungent smell of flowers and incense, giving the place a stirring atmosphere, a mixture of gay festival and a deep, sincere religious fervour.

The Temple had three levels, with a copy of the Granth being read on each of them. The priests continued this reading for twenty-four hours a day throughout the year.

Surinder quietly pointed out the beauty of the Temple, its thirty-one silver pillars and the beautiful inlay work which rivals the Taj Mahal. We visited all three floors and slowly wound our way down again, then continued our circuit of the tank.

At the opposite end of the tank, we passed a flight of steps where people were washing in the Holy Water to take away disease. Outside the temple precinct we removed the handkerchiefs, then re-washed our feet and collected our boots. Surinder suggested we spend the night in the Sikh Hostel.

The place seemed to be closed when we arrived and after wandering about for ten minutes, we found the man on night duty and booked in. This is one of the most unusual hostels I have ever, or ever will, stay in. It is typically Sikh in that it is open to people of all races, colours and creeds who may shelter and eat there free of charge during their stay is Amritsar. We were given our room number and pushed our way through the beggars hanging round the doors and proceeded to the second floor of the three-storied building. Surinder said goodnight, and told us he would see us in the morning.

We were told we were to share a room with another chap and had just finished fixing our beds when the door opened and a redheaded German entered. We introduced ourselves, then Karl exploded at us in broken English, telling us how he had been robbed in Tehran, going on to curse the Indian living conditions. It was some time before he simmered down, and finally went to bed.

I was unable to get much sleep that night because of the humidity and the noise from the street below, where merchants were shifting loads on their donkeys. We had a quick cleanup in a foul smelling bathroom, collected our gear and left our sleeping German. We were eating a chappatis breakfast when Surinder arrived with the official Temple guide to show us the Temple in daylight.

We washed our feet again, but this time were given special yellow cloths to cover our heads, a symbol of health and prosperity. We again stepped onto the shining marble tiles and looked across at the Temple. The copper gilt made us blink as it glittered in the bright sunlight, making a striking contrast to the deep blue sky and the white marble base. This time we were given candy to eat instead of the sweetmeats as we entered. We completed our conducted tour of the Temple and were then taken to the community kitchen which serves the Hostel and any others who desire or need a meal.

The kitchen was enormous and at one end had two huge open wood fires for cooking. A dozen women, quietly chanting, sat close by rolling out chapattis and tossing them on to an eight feet diameter hot plate to cook. When cooked they were stacked ready to feed hundreds of hungry mouths later in the day. On a second fire, candy was being made in a giant cooking pot, then laid out to cool on trays ... ...

*****

After a visit to the Sikh museum and art gallery, Surinder said he must be on his way and put in an appearance at work, so thanking him for his hospitality we shook hands and departed.

Turkish Gate at Lucknow

The Taj Mahal at Agra

Sikh Golden Temple at Amritsar, Punjab

Local transport

Lahore, Pakistan

CHAPTER SEVEN

Leaving India, Keith very nearly had his transistor radio confiscated by a customs officer. However, after a battle he managed to retain his radio but vowed he was going to get rid of it at the first opportunity as it had caused him enough trouble,

Keith had not long to wait, for on our second day in Lahore we were passing a wireless shop when he said to me,

"I wonder if I could unload the transistor here?"

"You can have a go," I said.

Keith asked for the manager and told him what he wanted, and the manager in return, eyed Keith with great suspicion saying,

"Where did you get it?"

"Singapore, and it isn't stolen," said Keith with a hurt expression.

The manager asked if he could borrow it, then took it into a back room to have it examined. He returned.

"I will give you three hundred rupees for it."

Keith looked at me and I shook my head.

"Four hundred," said Keith.

After some hot bargaining the price was settled at 350 rupees, giving Keith a 200 per cent profit on the deal.

We left quickly in case the manager changed his mind. We felt half inclined to return to Singapore to load up with more transistors for sale in Pakistan.

That same afternoon we were befriended by a group of Pathans who took us to dinner and insisted we go to the cinema afterward. It seemed hard to believe that the forefathers of these big, good-natured men were once the terror of the north-west frontier.

As a city we liked Lahore very much with its wide boulevards, spacious parks and gardens, and its friendly, small-town atmosphere. We visited the usual tourist features including the Fort, Mosques and the Shalamar Gardens, then on the fourth day made plans for our departure.

We were planning to take the northern route across Afghanistan via the Kyber Pass, but unfortunately our visas were cancelled because of border troubles, leaving us with no alternative but to take the Bolan Pass route. This also had its advantages. There was an agent for "Rabbit" motor scooters in Karachi and we would be foolish not to pay them a visit and have our scooter overhauled before tackling the desert.

Fifty miles south of Lahore, we left the green belt and entered the parched, desolate plains, which were broken for us by a visit to Harrappa, the most northerly city of Indus civilisation which reached its peak around 2000 BC.

The resident archaeologist met us and invited us to cool off on the verandah with a drink of water.

"I don't get many visitors," he said, "and most of those that do come always seem to be in a hurry. Where are you from?"

He eventually got around to showing us the small museum which had only just been started.

"Our collection is not very big yet, but we have a fair representation of their arts and crafts. A lot of it is pottery and much of it still bears its original brown glaze. The Indus people were in the Bronze Age as you can see by these well-preserved spearheads. We have very few of their farming implements so far. Here is some personal, semi-precious jewellery. They must have been – how do you call it? – stone carvers. See they carved many animals, cats, sheep, cattle and even birds.

"Come, I will take you to the excavations. They are not as large as Mohenjodaro's, but nevertheless just as interesting. The excavations were started in 1921 and now cover an area six and a half miles in circumference. People always think of the Sumerians being smart because they built in sun-dried bricks and the Egyptians because they used stone. But the Indus people made kiln-dried bricks – all of which measured 11 inches by 5 inches by 2 inches. In fact, they were ahead of many people today, for every house had drainage and sewerage which ran into drains under the street."

"Where did they come from originally?" I asked.

"We believe they were village tribesmen from the hills of Baluchistan and migrated to the valley about 5000 years ago. They were joined by others from the Iranian plateau and the two combined to make the civilisation. Their chief crops were wheat and cotton."

"What brought their civilisation to an end?"

"We are not sure, but we think they were overrun by the Aryans from the Iranian Plateau and south eastern Europe and were finally massacred."

We shuffled around the ruins looking at grinding stones and silos and occasionally unearthing pieces of broken pottery and eroded bronze fragments.

Harrappa had been well worth the visit. For a people living 4000 years ago, it had been a remarkable achievement.

The road was busy with camel trains and innumerable donkeys and because of this we were very late reaching Moultan. The ancient city was no more than a rubble heap and we had to hold our breath as we drove along the crowded, foul-smelling streets. We skidded across slime-covered gutters into the centre of the city where we were forced to a stop, by milling crowds who attacked our rucksacks, trying to open them. It was only by force, that we were able to get through the hordes and escape.

We asked the first policeman we met where we could put up for the night and were directed to the Aziz Hotel. The Aziz was a little beyond our present means but on enquiring, we found that the Dak Bungalow was next door, so we moved in for the night.

Before crossing the Chenab River early next morning, I had my camera carefully examined and was told not to take any photographs as the Barrages were in a military area. We spent the rest of the day criss-crossing canals and barrages. We did not mind this for at least there were trees shading the road for most of the way, making travel a little more comfortable.

As the sun touched the western horizon we began scouting for a campsite. It seemed as though we were never going to locate one when suddenly Keith said,

"What's that building off to the left?"

"Looks like a fort – or a police station," I said.

"Wonder if they take boarders?" said Keith.

"I don't know, let's find out," and I swung the scooter into the driveway.

We were met by the sergeant who addressed us in Urdu, but when he realised we spoke English he disappeared into the fort and returned with the sub-inspector, the man in charge.

"From where are you coming?" he asked.

We told him and asked if he knew a place where we could spend the night.

"Go no further, you must stay with us, be my guests."

Speaking in Urdu, he ordered the Sergeant to get Mirrabooka inside. The Sergeant screamed orders to four constables nearby and Mirrabooka was carried over the threshold and placed gently in the centre of the courtyard. The Police station was a true fort with high fortified mud walls and a jail at the rear, set between the barracks and the officer's quarters. The inspector apologised for not being able to offer us something better, but seemed happy when we told him we did not mind sleeping under the stars in the courtyard.

While we unpacked, two constables were sent to draw water for our bath. We washed in a box-like room, which was in reality a cell, and then returned to the courtyard, much refreshed.

"Leave everything for my men to fix. Come, we will drink tea," said the inspector.

Just outside the heavy front doors a table and four chairs had been set up on a small, but well kept lawn.

We sipped tea and watched the last of the light disappear in the western sky. The evening became pleasantly cool, and was soon smelling fresh from early falling dew.

Hurricane lamps now lit the courtyard and in the centre two beds had been set up complete with blankets and pillows. A large table and three chairs had been placed between them.

"Be seated," the inspector said.

He clapped his hands. One of has men trotted out from the barracks with a huge tray covered with a white cloth. The cloth was removed to display bowls of rice, chappatis, cutlets and a variety of curries.

We later found that the Inspector had dispatched one of his men to his wife in the village to get her to prepare this meal for us, while he had kept us busy outside the fort. We ate the welcome meal even though our poor stomachs revolted against the curry. When the meal was finished, the Inspector produced a vintage model radio and set it up on the table for our entertainment. Keith turned in and it was not long before he was asleep, buried deep in the blankets.

I managed to tune into a short wave concert programme and was accompanied by Brahm's First Symphony while I caught up on some writing. The night grew cold and I lost no time in seeking refuge in the warm blankets. I lay there for some time gazing up at the star-filled sky, listening to the rest of the concert programme while in the background, native drums beat in the nearby village. Sleep finally caught up with me and I switched the radio off and drifted into the land of nod.

I must have been asleep for several hours when something woke me. I opened my eyes to see steel glinting in the moonlight, about a foot from my eyes.

My first impulse was to leap out of bed but as my eyes shot upwards I saw it was one of the guards leaning over, scrutinising me. As soon as he realised I was awake, he stepped back smartly and stood at attention a few feet away. I raised myself on one elbow and shone my torch on him and he quickly disappeared in the direction of the big doors. Feeling a little disturbed, I settled back to sleep.

I was wide-awake at first light, and dressed just as the Inspector appeared on the scene with a constable carrying our breakfast on a tray. I told him of my visitor through the night and smiling he said,

"Yes, he in particular was most curious about you and your friend and no doubt thought it a good time to have a closer look.

"I wish he would have done it without the bayonet poking in my face," I replied.

"Would you like to stay with us for another three or four days?" the Inspector inquired.

"It would be nice, and thanks for the offer, but we have to get to Karachi."

Looking most hurt, he called on his men to help persuade us to stay. We finally convinced the dismal group of policemen that we should go and so, shaking hands all round, we departed.

The road ran parallel with the Indus and the country was flat and swampy, and the villages smelt foul from the stagnant water and lack of sanitation. We had been unable to buy any food so on coming to a large village we pulled in to see what we could find.

In the market place amongst the adobe dwellings, Keith spotted a stall carrying mandarins and went to make a purchase. He picked out six of the best and asked how much in sign language, then counted out the correct money to the man. He was about to climb on to the pillion when the man grabbed him and pulled him back yabbering savagely at him. Keith shook him off.

"You have got your money, now buzz off."

A crowd had now gathered and they all pressed in on Keith talking loudly and waving their arms around.

"Wonder what Keith has done?" I thought as I pushed my way through to him. The fruit man looked as though he would burst a blood vessel. The veins stuck out on his neck as he raved. Suddenly the fruit man bit the coins, then threw them at Keith. We picked them up and examined them and suddenly it occurred to us – they were counterfeit!

The noise of the crowd had reached a crescendo and we had to do something quickly. I dug into my pocket and pulled out replacements and a tip and handed them to the fruit man. He snatched the money out of my hand, chewed on it, spat it on the ground and then stormed off.

We wasted no time in getting back to the scooter and on our way, running the gauntlet of the hissing mob.

It was almost sunset before we came to a town with a reasonable char house where we could get a meal. The street was crowded and the loud speakers of the radios were making the air vibrate.

We had just seated ourselves at a table when all the radios were switched off, and from the direction of an isolated minaret came the wailing voice of the muezzin calling the faithful to prayer. Even the muezzin had been caught up in the in the modern age, he was standing at the base of the minaret using an amplifier system.

As we sipped our tea, we were watched by an audience of fifty or more. It was like feeding time at the zoo. When we had finished, two young men pushed out of the crowd,

"From where are you coming?"

They were students from Hyderabad and seemed most

concerned about our welfare.

"Where will you sleep tonight?" one of them asked.

"Somewhere south of here, beside the road" Keith said.

"No, no, that will be bad for you. Come, you will stay at our house."

Keith and I looked at each other and shrugged our shoulders.

"I'll get Mirrabooka and follow," I said.

The high altitude Persian Camels

Boys from Baluchistan

'We passed long lines of them striding along the hot bitumen ...'

The house lay behind a maze of narrow alleyways where a singsong was being conducted. Getting Mirrabooka under lock and key proved to be a near impossibility, but after much effort we conquered the tiny passageways and parked "Mirra" in a dingy adobe room. Our room had an earth floor and bamboo ceiling with mud stalactites hanging through the cracks. The doors and windows were heavily barred and the place looked more like a prison than a home.

Four men were sitting round a table, playing cards. One of the boys made a speech to them in Urdu, finishing it with introductions, then they packed up and went to find another room in which to carry on their game.

We packed at daybreak and got ready for the road, pleased to be away from the putrid sanitation, which was far worse than the Hooghly villages.

We passed over the Lloyd Barrage which lies just east of Sukkur and with the exception of camels, donkeys and women in purdah, there was little traffic. The women in purdah fascinated Keith and me with their long white calico hoods which covered them from head to toe, for they looked more like ghosts gliding over the ground than sturdy human beings. Their only ventilation was a four by two inch gauze set in the hood at eye level.

We reached Hyderabad at midday and rode into the old Sind Capital. Whenever I think of Hyderabad, I think of air conditioning systems, for all the buildings have tall air ducts up to fifteen feet high on each roof facing into the prevailing winds, giving the city a distinctive skyline ... ...

*****

We were on our way out of the city when heavy rain started to fall and we were forced to take shelter. It was not long before the smooth, oil-caked bitumen was greasy, reminding me of a certain stretch of road in Ceylon.

When the rain ceased, we got under way again but had not gone very far when I felt the wheels starting to skid.

"Hang on," I yelled to Keith. "It's on again."

I had hardly got the words out when the wheels slipped from underneath us and we were deposited bottoms first on the bitumen. We retained our sitting attitudes and slid gracefully along on our seats, travelling parallel with the scooter until we came to rest twenty yards further along the road. Unscathed we got to our feet. I switched the motor off, then wheeled Mirrabooka to the side of the road under a hail of applause from a group of onlookers who were nearly splitting their sides laughing.

We were dogged by rain all afternoon and forced to stop several times. Two miles from Thatta we came to Makli Hill, known as the Silent City because of its one million graves which cover an area of six square miles. We paused to have a closer look at the tiled graves which had carved headstones, some of them quite colourful.

On entering the ancient city of Thatta, we pulled up in front of a char house where we were immediately descended on by beggar boys calling for baksheesh and offering to polish the scooter for us.

Ignoring them, we drank our glass of tea then returned to the scooter where the beggars descended on us once again. One energetic beggar had actually made an attempt to polish Mirrabooka and as an example to the others we flipped him a coin which he grabbed, then ran off. The others screamed baksheesh as we mounted – and pelted handfuls of dirt over Mirrabooka, abusing us in their own language and bits of English they had learned. We rode out of Thatta in a cloud of dust as we were chased and bombarded with dirt and stones.

Fifty-seven miles from Karachi, we made camp and after a raisin breakfast next morning, set off across the sand hills to the city.

We joined a Super Highway and for the first time for a long while I was able to sit back and enjoy the ride into city. We passed the big international airport and from here on we were caught up in the wave of civilisation again. There was a variety of traffic, American and Continental cars, camel carts decorated with bells, donkey carts, cycle rickshaws, scooter taxis and horse drawn carriages.

Making enquiries, we navigated our way to our motor scooter agent, Sky Lines, and introduced ourselves to a bespectacled man in the office.

"Ah! I have been expecting you. I am Mr. Abid Khandwala. Sit down. Will you have tea?"

We were on our second cup when his second brother, Mr. Noor Khandwala, entered and we had to start all over again.

"You will be our guests while you are in Karachi," Abid said, "and do not hesitate to let us know if there is anything you want. You must be tired, so take a complete rest for the day. Come, we will book you into the Y.M.C.A. until we can settle you."

For roommates we had two Germans, a Spaniard and an American. In all an interesting bunch and company for Keith who was confined to bed with a dysentery attack for a day.

Sky Line's mechanic was most intrigued with my mending of the throttle cable.

"I would like some of the wire the throttle cable was fixed with. Have you got any?"

That was the last we saw of our welding wire.

The Khandwala family was determined to give us the best of Pakistani hospitality and towards the end of our stay, Keith and I were invited to Abid's home for dinner. The entire family from Grandfather to the children were gathered there to greet us and after introductions, we adjourned to the dining room where a Pakistani feast had been prepared for us.

"As you are the guests you will have the honour of commencing the meal," Abid said.

The table was packed with a variety of strange foods and neither Keith nor I had the slightest idea where we should start.

"You go first," Keith whispered.

"You would! Well, here goes," I muttered.

We were to eat with our hands and from here on I put my foot in it – twice.

Being a natural left hander, I forgot I was in a Muslim household and picked up a chop in my left hand. The dining room hushed. Suddenly I could see myself standing there with a chop in the wrong hand. I hurriedly switched it to may right hand at the same time apologising to everyone. Abid leaned forward and said,

"It is alright, but we also start with the sweets and not the meat."

"Oh!" I said, then reverently returned the chop to the plate and carefully picked up a sweet from another plate which had been pushed in front of me.

Everyone now relaxed. If I was going to survive the Muslim countries, I had better get used to eating right-handed and quickly. Calf skull soup was next on the menu and fortunately we were given a spoon. This was followed by rice, chops – which I had already fingered, fried bananas, various curries and chappatis. To finish the meal we were handed some tasty morsels to nibble, of their identity, I have no idea.

A gleaming, freshly painted "Rabbit" scooter was waiting on our arrival at the garage the following morning and the mechanic could not wait to get it on to the road to try it out.

"Come with me?" he asked, "I will see what she will do."

I had barely touched the pillion seat, when rubber burnt on the bitumen as we took off like a rocket. I clung on for dear life, not being used to speeds over forty-five mph, especially on an unloaded scooter. Somehow we returned safely to the garage where Keith greeted me with a grin.

"How do you like riding pillion?"

"No thanks. I've been driving for too long."

We packed early next morning and rode to "Sky Lines" where we were forced to unpack as the brothers had bought us a large quantity of supplies and it meant we had to reorganise our load.

Apart from the three gallons of water in water bags on the front and the two extra gallons of petrol, we now had spare parts, extra tools, and enough food to get us to Quetta and beyond, including a large box of sandwiches. I hesitated for a moment, wondering where I was going to put it all, but after a little urging from the brothers and the mechanic we somehow found room. Poor Mirrabooka was almost invisible under the great load, but there was one consolation, at least the sandwiches would be gone by evening.

As a final gesture, Abid handed us a letter of introduction to their cousin in Quetta and told us that he was a garage proprietor and was expecting us. We thanked them for their overwhelming hospitality and set forth on another stage.

The day was hot and dry and we soon lightened the weight by drinking water and at lunchtime eating a few sandwiches.

Next morning we crossed the Lloyd Barrage which is the largest of its kind in the world, with one of its canals eighty miles long and four to six miles wide. The entire canal system runs for some 6,500 miles. Oxen trudging in circles turned great paddle wheels to irrigate the individual paddy fields.

We paused at Sukkar long enough to cool off, for apart from the railway workshops and an enormous biscuit factory there seemed to be little else in the old walled city.

The glare almost had me asleep just when a shady plump of trees loomed up. We parked the scooter, spread out the ground sheet in the shade and in no time we were both sound asleep.

Suddenly something disturbed me and I woke up to see a tall turbaned figure standing over me.

"Hello," I said.

He mumbled something in Urdu, then ran off towards a shed and returned smartly with two other men each carrying a water bag. It was obvious they thought we had collapsed from the heat and now they were going to revive us. Neither of us felt particularly thirsty but we could not refuse their offer so we drank, letting them know it was much appreciated. They stayed with us until the heat of the day passed, talking to us in sign language and offering us betel nut to chew.

We rode off into the western sun and after a good run arrived at Jacobobad in the evening.

West of the town we had our first taste of real desert. As far as the eye could see the country was perfectly flat and devoid of all vegetation. Making the most of the cool, star filled night we rode on for another sixty miles before making camp on the seemingly endless plain. An icy cold wind was now blowing from the south-west so we parked Mirrabooka at our heads for a windbreak and lost no time getting into our sleeping bags.

I woke at first light and opened a pair of sleepy eyes. The cold wind was still blowing across the desert and made me snuggle deeper into my sand-covered sleeping bag.

Suddenly I heard a faint tinkling of bells and with an effort I rolled over onto my side to see silhouetted against the blood red dawn a long camel train shifting a nomad Afghan tribe back into the mountains for the summer. They moved gracefully across the skyline. The only sound above the wind was the gentle tinkling of the camel bells. We lay there fascinated until the cavalcade had passed, then coming back to reality, set about getting ourselves on the road.

Approaching the Bolan Pass we entered Baluchistan and almost straight away noticed a marked change in the appearance of the people. Both men and women seemed dress-conscious, with the women especially looking quite colourful in their long flowing red robes and baggy trousers. Between villages we passed long lines of them striding along on the hot bitumen, with the women carrying the loads.

We began to climb, then suddenly out of nowhere we came upon the crystal clear waters of the Morad River. From here on the country improved slightly as the road followed the river up through a broad, red and yellow sandstone gorge which stood out against the deep blue sky. As we climbed, the colours grew richer and the gorge narrowed to a funnel and a strong wind started to buffet us, making it hard for me to keep the scooter upright. The railway joined the road and the pass tightened and high up on the steep cliff walls one could see ancient lookout towers that once guarded this gateway to India. We thought of all the conquering armies that had marched across the deserts of Persia and had fought their way through the pass to the plains of the sub-continent.

We made a final ascent between the fortified sheer cliff walls and then dropped into a broad green valley where we received the full force of the Sistan Winds. Riding became dangerous as we were all but lifted off the road by the blasts.

The 5,500 feet Quetta Plateau became cold and bleak and we had to stop and rug up before going any further.

Quetta, which was razed by an earthquake in 1935, today shows little evidence of the disaster. We rode past briskly walking people to the address we had been given and discovered that Mr. Khandwala's garage fronted the city bus depot where we drove between an odd assortment of bus passengers lounging around on boxes and worn out tyres.

Mr. Khandwala was in his office waiting for us.

"Welcome to Quetta, I have been expecting you. I received an airmail letter from my cousins yesterday telling me about you. Sit down."

Tea and sandwiches were brought, then Mr. Khandwala said,

"Now what sort of accommodation do you like?"

"Nothing too fancy," said Keith, "so long as it is comfortable."

We finished our tea then followed Mr. Khandwala across town to the tourist hotel, which turned out to be full.

"I am sorry," said Mr. Khandwala, "but we will have to try the Dak Bungalow. You should be right there. I know the manager."

We were shown a room with a fireplace in the corrugated iron building and asked if we liked it. It suited us nicely. It had two beds and a table and a small room at the back which we were told was the bathroom. The place was like an ice box and we wasted no time in asking for a load of firewood.

"I will leave you now," said Mr. Khandwala. "Call at the garage tomorrow and I will arrange for you to be taken into the hills."

We had breakfast next morning in the company of an Englishman named Jim, one of the best storytellers I have ever met. He had us spellbound until lunch time with tales of his game hunting experience in Bengal, Kashmir and the Sind, where he stood face to face with tigers, buffaloes, elephants and crocodiles.

"How long have you been hunting?" I said.

"Ever since the Income Tax people caught up with me in England," he replied.

For the next few days we were shown around the surrounding country in a Land Rover, courtesy of Mr. Khandwala who was doing everything possible to make our stay in Quetta an interesting one. We visited farms where rice, apples, apricots and citrus fruits were growing and were shown Quetta's new dam and other places of interest.

Dominating the skyline behind the city is a high, snow-capped mountain range with the 11,738 feet Mt. Zargum standing out above all. The country looked wild and rugged, and to us, most inviting. We told Mr. Khandwala we were going to climb the mountain and. he threw his hands up in horror,

"It is impossible," he said. "You will get lost and besides the leopards and bears are very dangerous."

We eventually talked him into it and he agreed to let us go on the condition that we return the same day. We agreed and he made arrangements for us to be dropped at the base of the mountain range at daybreak next day.

Sunrise found us driving across the trackless piece of country at the base of Mt. Zargum in Mr. Khandwala's Land Rover.

When the vehicle could go no further we jumped off and set out on the long climb. We were under a cloudless sky and we knew full well that the day would be a scorcher, clambering over the hard, boulder covered mountain. Scattered amongst the razor sharp rocks, which were already tearing at our boots, clusters of pink, blue and red and yellow wild flowers made a splash of colour against the orange coloured rock. At the top of the first ridge the country opened out into a saucer-like valley, on the other side of which was a red mountain wall capped with snow which dazzled in the sunlight. A flock of mountain sheep were being shepherded by two turbaned tribesmen who stared hard at us as we passed, and indicated to us to keep away from their hide tents which were close by.

We selected the only climbable ridge we could see along the mountain wall and then started the long slog up scree slopes. The scree ran out and we started to rock climb. The sun was nearing its zenith and we could feel ourselves being dehydrated as we scrambled around great ravines and gorges. Overhead, vultures and eagles circled and occasionally dive-bombed us – usually at a spot where we had little to hang on to.

It was 2 p.m. when we reached the snow line and ate our cut lunch before tackling the summit. The views were excellent even though there was a heavy heat haze. To the north we looked on to the rugged ranges that lay across the Afghani Border and to the south-west the long endless plain disappeared into the haze. Far down below on the other side, Quetta made a neat pattern in the lush valley.

We cooled off with some snow and refilled the water bottle from a stream before starting the descent. We were lucky in picking the right ridge and made a reasonably quick descent into the saucer valley. The western sun was full on us all the way down and by the time we reached the plain Keith's lips were badly cracked and swollen. We came on two tribesmen on the way who were travelling in the same direction as us, but unfortunately they did not hear us coming. One of them was loaded up with a great number of pots and pans and as soon as he saw us, stepped smartly back off the track and in the process lost his footing and sent his pots and pans clattering down the side of the mountain. His mate was carrying a load of timber and he too dropped his load on the spot and hid behind some rocks until we were out of sight. We offered to pick up some of the pots and pans but the man would have nothing to do with us.

It was dark when we reached the city and reported back to an anxious Mr. Khandwala who stared unbelievingly when we told him we reached the top.

On arrival at the Bungalow, Jim greeted us.

"I have a friend of yours here. He says he met you in Amritsar."

A red headed German stepped into the light.

"Remember me," he said greeting us like long lost friends.

"How are you?" we asked.

Looking most miserable, he told us he was penniless and barely had enough money to buy a chappati.

"Have you chaps eaten?" asked Jim.

"No, not yet," answered Keith.

"Good, would all three of you like to come to my place and we will have a slap-up feed?"

"Well ———" we said.

Jim's place turned out to be a battered old panel van parked under a large garage which was no more than a junk heap. Four Pakistanis also lived on the premises and it took little imagination to see that they thought the world of him.

"Make yourselves comfortable on that battered lounge suite while I prepare the grub," Jim said.

Two of the Pakistani boys went shopping, while Jim slaved over his paraffin stove turning out one of the best meals of steak and mashed potatoes I have ever seen. Jim showed us his panel van and for the first time I started to believe his hunting stories.

The van was a small armoury and was complete with skins.

Leaving Quetta was the hard part, for now Jim and his friends wanted us to stay on, but we had our visas ready for countries ahead. When it was time to leave, Mr. Khandwala filled our petrol tank and we said goodbye, then rode out along the beautiful tree lined avenues of Quetta for the last time.

It was not long before we were back in the desert country again, only this time the landscape was cluttered with giant, grey rocks that stood out on the skyline like headstones. On riding over the crest of a rise, we were startled to see two rucksacked figures walking along the road ahead of us.

"Where do you think you're going?" I called as I pulled up beside them.

"Home," was the reply.

"Doing it the hard way, aren't you?" I said.

Our two new friends were American boys making their way back to the States via Europe after two years in Japan. They thought we were crazy trying to ride the overloaded scooter across Persia and told us so.

"You will never make it, in fact you are bloody mad."

We returned the compliment and gave them a drink of water, telling them it was their last. Then, wishing them luck, rode off.

We arrived in Dalbandin next morning in time for breakfast at the Dak Bungalow. Dalbandin is the last outpost in west

Pakistan, except for the customs near the border, and consisted mainly of a mud fort in the centre of a large palm grove. Just to make sure, we refuelled from four gallon tins at the fort then set off to the border.

Ten miles from Dalbandin the bitumen finished and we bounced off along the start of a long grey road. The road was a mixture of sand and shingles and our speed dropped to between ten and fifteen miles per hour. As the sun reached its zenith, the heat and glare became terrific and mirages common. Skids were frequent, and I gradually took the role of a dirt track rider. The small wheels with the great weight up top were now showing a distinct disadvantage for every time we hit a soft patch they would burrow in and stop the scooter dead in its tracks. Falls were numerous and on two occasions we were pitched headlong over the handlebars into the grey dust.

A strong dust storm sprang up and forced us to take shelter beside a group of mud houses. I parked Mirrabooka, then sat against the wall to have a snooze, leaving Keith to keep an eye on things.

I was woken by the sound of voices and saw a group of villagers standing around us, giving us betel nut smiles. One of the men stepped forward and in sign language asked us if we wanted some tea. We nodded, and he prodded a little man who got busy and stoked up the dung fire. Strong syrupy teas were served to us in two very small cups and as we drank the villagers talked and giggled amongst themselves, obviously enjoying a joke at our expense. Our crash helmets had them fascinated and we had a hard job retaining them.

It was not until later that night that we discovered the villagers had robbed us of all our food while we were busy drinking the tea they had so generously provided.

The dust storm increased in ferocity and by the time we reached Nok Kuindi we were being sandblasted. Ten miles from Nok Kuindi we were battling along at a steady twenty miles per hour when we hit another soft patch and we were both propelled through the air. This time I came off second best, for on the way over the handlebars I gave my right shin a terrific wallop and in no time it was like a football. The leg was most painful and I had difficulty in working the brake, let alone using it for an outrigger.

As soon as we entered Nok Kuindi we made for the police station to see about getting cleared through Customs. I had parked Mirrabooka and was hobbling to the gate with Keith when a man dressed in a smart, lightweight suit called out to me in English and asked what was the matter with my leg. When I told him, he said he was a visiting doctor and asked if he could have a look at it.

"Hmm. If you can stand the pain, I will try and break up the clot before it settles," he said.

"Okay, go ahead," I said. I lay down on the sand while he got to work with the palm of his hand, rubbing and pushing. He was not fooling about it being a painful operation, but in ten minutes he had the swelling down and I was able to hop around in reasonable comfort. With Mirrabooka cleared through Customs, we rode to the Dak Bungalow to discover our red headed German waiting for us.

"How did you get here?" we asked.

"I got a lift on a truck last night. I will try and reach Tehran. I have friends there."

We shared our chappatis and rice with him until the dust storm drove us to our rooms.

The wind howled all night and made the old building shudder and by morning we found ourselves carpeted in a layer of grey dust. When the storm had died down sufficiently we set out to cross the eighty-four miles of near trackless sand hills which separated us from the Persian border.

1921 Digs at Harappa, Pakistan

Entrance to the Bolan Pass

The Bolan Pass – 'Entrance to the Prehistoric'

Mosque in Pakistan

Looking down on Quetta in Pakistan, from Afghanistan

Towards Quetta in Pakistan, from Afghanistan

CHAPTER EIGHT

I was squinting into the western sun and concentrating on the road and handlebars when I heard a sudden crack! crack! and a whining noise. Keith leaned forward and screamed in my ear.

"Pull up. There are two soldiers with rifles chasing us!"

I glanced in the rear vision mirror and saw two khaki clad figures carrying rifles running flat out after us.

I wasted no time in coming to a halt. As soon as they reached us and got their breath back they gave us a burst of language in Persian, at the same time pointing their rifles at us in a menacing manner. We had never heard Persian spoken before and the sound of these two excited tongues made it very difficult to understand what the trouble was about.

After five minutes, we worked out what it was. Apparently we had driven past their frontier post situated on top of one of the big sand hills. They were both young and raggedly dressed in battered uniforms. One of them had two stripes on his arm and by the way he was carrying on, he was trying to get three. Screaming loudly, they demanded to see our passports, so we pulled them out. Keith's was nearly snatched from his fingers as it came out of his pocket. I showed them mine but refused to let them touch it, for I had the feeling, if they got their hands on the passport it would be the last time I would see it.

They became very excited again and I quickly made signs and asked where the Customs were. The Corporal pointed down the road.

"Come on, let's go," I said, mounting Mirra and indicating that we were going to the Customs.

They understood what we meant and simmered down slightly, but now demanded a ride on the scooter to the Customs which was about three miles away. The Corporal had one leg over the tail rack when I twisted the throttle, leaving him standing on one leg in a cloud of dust.

I stopped in front of the walled Custom building and waited for the two puffing and perspiring soldiers.

At that moment a big, black American car pulled up and a smartly dressed Persian got out.

"Customs?" I asked.

We were in luck, he understood.

"Yes, this is the place. Have you been having trouble with the guards?"

"Yes."

With that, he took up the battle for us and abused the guards in the language they understood, then dismissed them.

It took us about an hour to get cleared through Customs,

filling in papers and having Mirra checked, and by the time we were finished we were beginning to wonder about the freedom of the country which had been promised to us at the Persian Embassy in Delhi.

It was a relief to get away from the Customs and get back onto the open road.

We had dinner of raisins and water as the sun set, and then we climbed into our sleeping bags and took refuge from the wind. The night was as clear as crystal, and from across the wastes the howling of jackal packs could be heard on the wind.

We arrived at our first Persian town, Zahedan, early next morning and for the first time in my life I had to officially drive on the right hand side of the road. At an intersection we were waved through by a pretty policeman dressed in a Royal blue uniform splattered with gold braid. I drove around the corner and parked by a teahouse with the intention of getting some breakfast, but we were immediately surrounded by a big crowd.

I jerked the scooter onto its stand, but was forced to hang on to it as the crowd tried to tip it over. I was wondering what we were going to do to quiet them, when the constable on duty by the traffic lights and two other policemen came to our rescue, making a batons charge on the mob, laying into them with their truncheons. Several youths went down for the count and were trampled by the retreating mob, which formed a large circle at a safe distance.

We thanked the policemen, and then asked them if they would watch our scooter while we went to get something to eat. They nodded and two of them stood guard on the scooter while the other escorted us to the teahouse.

Zahedan is the rail head link with Pakistan and once a week the water train comes from Quetta and also carries passengers and sometimes cars across the desert to Zahedan. From here, overland passengers usually catch a bus to take them on the long haul to Tehran.

With a full load of petrol, water and food, we mounted and rode out of town. The road at first was good gravel and travelled over flat country bordering Afghanistan. We reached the road junction where one road forks northward to Meshed and the other west towards Kerman. We made our decision and took the one to Kerman as we wanted to visit Isfrahan and probably Shiraz – if the road was not too bad.

We turned due west and then started on the long climb up over the Koal Band Range. The country was devoid of all vegetation but the colours of the sand and rocks were wonderful and ranged through reds, oranges and yellows to greens and mauves. There were plenty of mirages but we were really taken in with one which seemed to be a beautiful fast flowing stream which crossed the road.

It turned out to be real and I pulled up while Keith went to investigate. He bent down and scooped up a handful and tasted it, but smartly spat it out – it was salt. Along the water's edge were a number of skeletons of animals that had fallen victim to the water. We had been drinking our share of water and now our hopes of refilling the bags, for the present, were dashed.

The descent of the range was colourful but precarious as the steep grades were deep in sand. Crossing valleys, we were surprised to see beautifully marked deer and an occasional fox.

We filled our water bags from a spear pump at an army post, then set off across a seemingly never-ending plain. Our speed dropped again as we started ploughing through soft sand.

Toward sunset we came upon a nomad camp by the roadside and were waved down by two wild-looking tribesmen. In sign language, we were invited to come and sit by the fire. Wondering what was in store for us, we accepted the invitation and sat down, cross-legged, on a large carpet and waited. We had not long to wait for a camel appeared, loaded up with four great barrels of water, being led by a tribesman. It looked as though we had been invited to share tea with them and as soon as the camel knelt down and was unloaded, a large iron pot was filled with water and placed on the fire. Tea was made and we were handed bowls of the brew plus a large lump of sugar which had been chipped off a great stick of sugar about the size of a baseball bat. We were not aware of their custom and dropped our sugar into the cup and began stirring it with my penknife. Not until we noticed the nomads' expressions did we realise that we had done the wrong thing. The headman demonstrated how the tea should be drunk. Placing the lump of sugar in his mouth, he sipped the tea till the sugar was dissolved, then replaced it with more ... ...

*****

We made camp on a treeless, sandy plain under the star-filled sky and felt completely isolated, there being no visible sign of life in any form.

We were sitting back, relaxing, having a late supper of tea and chappatis, when we heard a sudden scampering noise close by.

It sounded like a large animal.

We grabbed our torches and switched them on. Standing in the beams about ten feet away from us was a jerboa, a little animal about four inches high resembling a kangaroo. It was standing on two spindly hind legs and when we shone the torch on it, it turned and cocked its mouse-like head at us as much as to say,

"So what? I was here first."

It stood there waving its long, whip-like tail and rubbing its face with its short fore-paws. We threw it some pieces of chappati and it bounced over to them picked them up and gnawed at them. Apparently they were not up to standard for it threw them back at us. As soon as we switched the torches off, it started careering madly around the camp – and went as far as jumping on us. We were not too sure if it was pleased to see us or if it wanted us to get out. We played games with it for about an hour but could not stand the pace and finally gave up and retreated into our sleeping bags.

All night long we had the pleasure, and later the displeasure, of its company as it bounced over us, trying to get into our sleeping bags. Keith reached a point where he had had enough. He sat up in his sleeping bag and picked up the machete, threatening to chop the jerboa's head off if it came back again. It didn't, however, and Keith went back to sleep. With our ears on the ground, his feet pounding the sand sounded more like a herd of elephants than a jerboa.

We rose at first light and packed up in the red dawn. Even the grey sand turned red for the first hour of the day. Ahead of us was the finish of the 300 mile dry stretch. As the sun climbed high in the sky, the heat of the day mounted and by mid-morning we were riding along the breezeless plain, in temperatures well over a hundred degrees.

All around us were mirages, some in the form of great castles and penthouses but in reality they were often only slabs of jagged rock, sometimes no more than four feet high. Blasts of hot air hit us and we could almost feel ourselves evaporating. Our lips were starting to swell and crack and water stops became frequent. Keith was finding it hard to stay awake in the glare of the day and by midday, our bodies were about the same colour as the ground we were travelling over. Giant scorpions crossed our path with their big upturned tails waving over them in a menacing attitude. The scorpions were monsters and made us feel uncomfortable when we thought of how we had been sleeping in the open.

The fuel gauge was reading 'Empty' and there was no sign of habitation. Our water was also low, as the very air we breathed seemed to be on fire.

Suddenly, in the distance, another mirage appeared, this time in the form of an oasis complete with palm trees and buildings. It was not until we got quite close that we realised that the mirage was Bam. An overloaded scooter that was nearly out of petrol and carrying two grimy passengers spluttered its way down the narrow palm tree lined street. We rounded a curve between high mud buildings and there, straight in front of us in the centre of the road, was a battered old petrol wagon, almost completely blocking the road. The owner of the store had just refilled his forty-four gallon drums from the tanker but refused to sell us petrol under ten gallon quantities, telling us to go to another place if we wanted small quantities.

We had no choice. The road led into the main street, which was wide, tree-lined and had a number of modern shops. We made several stops to enquire the whereabouts of the garage but nobody seemed the least bit interested.

Suddenly a small boy rode up on a pushbike.

"Where is it you wish to go?" he said in precise English.

"Petrol," I said.

"Please follow me," he said, and pedalled off to stop under a shady tree in front of a narrow mud building.

I had hardly put the scooter on its stand when we were surrounded by the usual pack of local delinquents. They immediately tried to get into our rucksacks and Keith had a busy time keeping them at bay while I went to buy the petrol. All the men in the town were having a siesta and the boys were in charge. At first I refused to deal with this bunch, but when I realised that the men had no intention of stirring themselves I was forced to do business with the delinquent manager. The only information I could get out of the old man was the price, which worked out at eleven shillings a gallon. They knew only too well that if I did not buy at their price we would have to push the scooter the two hundred miles to Kerman.

I was now thankful that I was not driving a Cadillac.

We wasted no time in starting up and shaking ourselves free of this bunch of jackals. We had gone about fifty yards when I noticed the English-speaking boy chasing us on his cycle.

"Please, Sirs - excuse my countrymen - they are a bad lot. Would you like to see the 2,000 year old Bam Fort?"

"Yes, which way do we go?"

"Follow me," he said and rode off at a breakneck speed.

We were led along narrow, winding streets just wide enough to allow us through, then we broke out onto the plain and there, in the distance, was the fort. A fort of this nature was something we had been hoping to see. It was one of those ancient mud fortresses that had been built near oases to guard them when they were vital keys to trade along the caravan routes.

The place was large with three rings of forty feet mud walls rising to a central castle on the top of which a lookout tower had been placed in recent years.

The boy told us he had never been allowed to go to the Fort as his father thought it unsafe because the old dwellings inside were in a state of collapse. I think our arrival had been just what he wanted: a chance to try out his English and an excuse to explore the old Fort.

We passed through the outer wall via the main gate and entered another world. Inside the first ring was a ruined adobe town where its hundreds of dwellings were slowly crumbling with decay. The second ring was more or less a defence area with fighting towers at regular intervals along the walls. The third ring, where the castle stood, was sealed off and there was no way of scaling the forty feet high walls. In its day the fort must have been an almost invincible stronghold. Scrambling through the ruins, Keith picked up several pieces of broken pottery that were almost buried in the dust of the collapsing walls.

I decided to get a better photo and climbed onto the outer wall. A large section of the parapet was still intact and from here I got fine view of the Fort and the oasis and Bam. It was easy to imagine the defenders fighting off invaders, showering the attackers with arrows from the slits in the wall ... ...

*****

I was mounting Mirra when I noticed water running onto the ground, and I leant over the front of the scooter to investigate. Keith and I were furious, for one of our water bags had been slashed beyond repair, more work of the local mob.

Outside Bam, we crossed the last of the plains and then

commenced our climb into the hills that eventually led us onto a ten thousand feet plateau. We made the mistake of trying to fill our remaining water bags from a deep fast flowing canal near a village and were chased off by the villagers, who threw stones at us.

The road curled up amongst the hills and had flattened into a valley when we saw a car pulled off the road ahead of us. Two blond-headed men were fussing about a Fiat 600 which had definitely seen better days. On the side of it 'Hamburg to Bombay' was written in big print. I stopped to see if we could be of any assistance and learnt that the Germans had bought the car new for the trip and had driven it from Hamburg to Bombay and were now on their way home. They were in trouble as all six of their tyres were worn almost to the canvas and they had no replacements. The suspension had completely collapsed and the motor was very sick. In general it was a wreck, but they were hoping to get it as far as Isfahan where they thought spare parts would be available. We gave them a hand trying to get the engine going until it got too dark, so we all then decided to make camp and forget about the troubles of the day.

I got Mirra onto the road next morning only to discover she had a flat front tyre. While I was effecting repairs, Keith went to help the boys. Half an hour later the Fiat's motor roared into life and with a wave from the Germans the car disappeared in a cloud of dust.

When the dust settled we followed across the plateau, which was very scenic for on either side of us towered fourteen thousand feet snow-capped peaks. Clouds crept across the sky and, as the temperature dropped, we had to dig out our wind jackets and gloves. About midday the sun came out and almost cooked us.

At this point a fast flowing, snow-fed stream swept towards the road and ran parallel. The sight of this beautiful clear water was too much for us and we decided to take a long overdue bath and get some of the caked dust off us. The stream was knee deep and ice cold and lush green grass grew along the banks. We had nearly finished when a cloud of dust appeared on the horizon. It was a truck.

There was no doubt about it, we could not even take a bath in peace. The big truck pulled up beside the scooter as we were getting dressed and the door opened and out jumped the driver, his two offsiders, and our red headed German.

"So you got dis far. We have been looking for you," he said, looking pleased to see us.

We were introduced to the truck driver and crew and then the driver invited us to join them for a meal twenty miles further on at a small village.

The place looked like a haunt for truckies, as three other trucks were pulled up outside a big stone building in the centre of the village. We entered the Persian version of an Indian char house and seated ourselves at one of the four feet high stone benches that took up each corner of the room. The benches were covered with thick carpets and made us feel more like sleeping than eating. Truckies were sitting cross-legged on the carpets eating bowls of rice, mutton and vegetables and dripping the thick gravy over them. The driver ordered for us and we were brought goosht (mutton), a variety of vegetables, and rice which we ate with our hands.

We said goodbye to the German and set off in the wake of the big truck but had only gone about ten miles when we had a puncture in the rear tyre. We unloaded and set about mending the puncture in the shadow of a big storm which was building up in the mountains. The mountains looked most spectacular shrouded in the jet-black mantle, and thunder boomed and echoed out across the valley. I had just finished operations when the heavens opened up and rain poured down. There was no shelter for miles so we donned our raincoats and crouched beside the scooter.

The rain eased off to a light drizzle and we got under way. The road was in an awful mess, for now the dust had turned to slush. There was one consolation however – we were going through before the runoff hit the road. As it turned out, the heavy trucks following us were not so lucky and were bogged for four days.

Nearing Kerman the country improved with crops of rice, maize and vegetables growing. Camels again became numerous, but they were a different breed from the Pakistani camel. These were high altitude camels, shorter and more hairy than their brothers of the plains.

We were within sight of Kerman when the rain started again, and this time it really teemed! I decided to make a run for it and we skidded and slewed our way into town to the first shop awning I could find. The deluge lasted for three quarters of an hour and by the time it had finished a river was flowing down the main street and into some of the shops. The annual rainfall for this area is about eight inches and it looked as though it had all fallen in the one day. We were about to move off to find a hotel when an English speaking Persian called us and asked,

"Where is it you want to go?"

"An hotel. Any suggestions?"

He gave us directions to what he described as the "Best hotel for you in Kerman."

We parked in front of the hotel entrance and went to

investigate. What we thought was the entrance was not, for inside the big double doors was a long, winding passageway of stone which led to a door at the other end. Behind this door was the hotel built in the form of a hollow square with a large fountain and pool in the centre of the square. The manager, a middle aged man dressed in whites, greeted us in English.

"How much do you wish to pay for a room?"

We told him a ridiculously low price.

He grinned, then said,

"I understand," and showed us to a room which was about fifteen feet square with a high, richly painted, domed ceiling.

"Will this suit you?" ... ...

We unpacked and sorted out our gear. Everything was caked with mud and white dust, so I made enquiries about the bathroom and was shown to a stone cellar deep under the hotel. The place was like one of those dungeons where people spent their time in chains, with water dripping on the stone slabs and rats running around.

We were eating dinner when there was a knock on the door and two boys entered dressed in baggy grey suits. The darker of the lads spoke,

"You are English?"

"No," I said.

"But you speak English, from where are you coming?"

The two boys were learning English at school and, making the most of the opportunity, had come to practise on us. The evening finished up as a language class with the boys teaching us Persian in return for us teaching them English.

After breakfast next morning, the boys returned to take us on a tour of Kerman. The day was humid after the previous day's rain and the boys insisted we walk in the shade of the trees and the shop awnings. We were taken to the market first, a huge affair with an enormous high dome in the centre. The market was divided by many alleys, between which merchants were selling carpets, clothing, fruit, vegetables, a large variety of nuts, and animals. This was the first large Persian market we had seen and we explored it thoroughly. Smith's alley was the noisiest place with craftsmen beating copper urns into shape with their hammers ... ...

In a nearby grinding mill, mangy, blindfolded, undersized camels walked round in endless circles, turning the great stones crushing the grain into flour. These beasts probably never saw the light of day as they were kept in the mill until they had outlived their usefulness.

The boys' uncle owned a carpet factory and with the boys acting as interpreters we were shown over the factory, a high, narrow, mud building. Two rows of workers were busy working on their own designs, chanting as they worked. The average time for one person to make a rug, we were told, was about four months, and that is working from daylight till dark, sometimes seven days a week. I remarked on the youth of the workers and was told that rug makers start when they are very young and are usually finished at twenty-five because they go blind. This was easy to understand, for this place relied only on the sun to provide the light through the high, narrow windows. The swift hands astounded me as they slipped along the rug, weaving another row and then beating it down tight with shaped wooden mallets. Most of the workers had deformed fingers through constant use in this manner ... ...

*****

Twenty miles from Kerman we came to the turnoff to Shiraz. Here we had to decide whether to take the main road to Yazd or the track across the wild country to Shiraz, which we had been advised not to do. Our next fuel point along this track was unknown and, as much as we wanted to see Persepolis, we decided to settle for the mosques of Isfahan. As it turned out we probably did the right thing, for later we found out that a group of surveyors had been robbed and killed while travelling that road at this time.

We were dogged by rain all day and in the later afternoon the landscape became spectacular, the foreground lit with a bright sun against a foreboding inky black sky. The mountains all around us echoed with the claps of thunder.

Just on sunset a cold wind sprang up bringing more rain with it, forcing us to seek shelter for the night.

In the last fading light, we spotted a derelict adobe hut fifty yards off the road, and swung off across the sandy flat and pulled up outside the old building. We forced the heavy, wooden, double doors and went in.

It was a long time since the place had been used and with the exception of a few cobwebs and a little grass on the earth floor, there was nothing. We checked the four rooms carefully to make sure we had no company in the way of scorpions and other vermin, and unloaded Mirrabooka and got her and our gear in out of the black night ... ...

*****

We liked Yazd. It is a picturesque town lying in the shadow of the big, snow-capped mountains. I think my most outstanding impression of the town was the enormous perforated chappatis that are made in the bakeries there and are called "Non". They are beaten out in the same manner as the Indian chappatis, except that they are three feet and over in diameter. Before being placed in a coke-fired oven, small stones about half an inch in diameter are pressed into the chappatis, and when baked they are removed by banging the chappatis on a board. The finished product is like a golden brown perforated doormat, which is then hung on nails outside the shop ready for the customers.

Persians also seem very fond of sugar, for almost every shop in Yazd had for sale great baseball-bat lumps of sugar dangling on the end of string. Smith's alley was again worth a visit – providing one had ear plugs.

From Yazd we travelled across a desert at the base of a high mountain range and by noon we were again being sand blasted by Seistan winds.

Between Yazd and Nain we passed through four villages that were isolated in the desolate sandy wastes making us wonder what kept people there. All these villages had one peculiar feature, their dwellings. The adobe houses were built in the form of a square and were all surrounded by a high mud wall. Their roofs were large adobe domes, smooth and symmetrical, and from a distance the houses looked like giant anthills. Some domes had holes in the top and were used for kitchens. In most cases the domes did not cover the entire roof but were flattened out around the base, before meeting the walls. The main doors into the houses were all of wood, big and heavy.

The road out of Nain rises about 1,500 feet before it starts to twist. The plateau is ringed with snow capped peaks and we passed little, walled villages surrounded by deep green paddy fields - seeming quite out of place in the surrounding brown plain.

2000 year-old, Mud & straw, Castle & Village at Bam, Persia

Oasis, South of Bam, Persia

Village near Kerman, Persia

South of Kerman — Bath-time with first of running water for 2 weeks

Coming into Yazd, Persia

In the City Square, just after breakfast, Yazd, Persia

CHAPTER NINE

Approaching Isfahan, the country was undulating, sandy desert and we were buffeted by parching winds all the way. The landscape was broken now and then by an occasional oasis and the earth ventilators of the underground water system, which was installed to bring water from the hills to the city.

Crossing a row of barren, rugged hills, we ran down to the valley on a broad, bitumen road lined with tall trees. The water tunnels emerged and emptied their contents into the canals which carried the water through the city. The sight of the green trees and running water was like a breath of fresh air.

My relaxation was short lived for the city proved to be a place of heavy traffic and hell drivers – maybe I had had a free hand on the road for too long. One consolation, the city was well laid out with spacious avenues and I had plenty of road on which to dodge about.

Isfahan was just as the tourist brochure described it, a city of parks and great mosques, the world's most colourful. The French influence could be seen in the city for as well as the cars and the second language (French), most of the streets had French names. We were advised to stay at the Anglican Mission, and after many attempts, finally found it.

The Mission took up a whole block and comprised a school boarding house, church, and spare rooms.

"Our accommodation is not first class, you understand, but if you don't mind sleeping in one of the unused class rooms you are welcome to stay," said the Bishop. "By the way don't leave anything lying around, the children are still learning."

It was good to have a place where we could unload and have plenty of room to reorganise our gear.

The night life was starting to stir when we stepped outside the walls of St. Lukes and, with the exception of the veiled women, the city reminded me very much of Paris.

The tourist season was in full swing and brightly-lit souvenir shops were displaying a great variety of articles. "Tourist Catchers", men employed by these shops, were a menace and would descend on passers by and literally drag them into the shop where they were obliged to buy, to get out. We avoided most of them, but we too, were eventually caught and dragged into a shop where salesmen descended on us. We had no intention of buying anything, but they were only too glad to get rid of us after we had almost emptied the shelves examining things.

We were buying peanuts from a vendor when a Persian approached us and insisted he show us the city by night. We almost walked the length and breadth of the city, including a few back alleys where we felt a little uncomfortable and kept a sharp lookout over our shoulders and a hand on our pockets.

"Would you like to try a Persian dinner?" he asked.

"Yes, suits me," said Keith, "I'm starving."

Not knowing what to expect I also agreed and we followed our guide to a place with high wooden doors. Our guide rapped on the door and a man opened it and we entered. The café was built in the usual hollow square with a fountain in the centre. A man in baggy trousers showed us to a table and our guide ordered for us. Ten minutes later the waiter reappeared with three big steaming bowls of rice and placed them in front of us. Next three raw eggs – still in their shells, were placed beside the bowls along with shallots, other green vegetables, some bowls of spice and blobs of curd. Our guide showed us what to do. Making a hole in the centre of the steaming rice, he broke the egg and emptied it into the rice then covered it with the hot rice and waited for it to cook. Shish-kebab, vegetables and curd were piled on top. The meal went down quite well but Keith was about halfway through his when he stopped.

"You can have these exotic, eastern dishes, I've about had them."

Our guide and waiter looked hurt, and I made the mistake of telling them how much I enjoyed it – and I had my plate filled again. I managed to eat a portion, then pushed the rest away feeling the same way as Keith.

On arrival at the Mission, we were surprised to see the two American hitchhikers we had met west of Quetta. Don, the shorter of the two said,

"We didn't expect to see you here. We felt sure you would have been bogged after all the rain."

Next morning the four of us turned tourist and made our first stop at the Royal Mosque, or the Maejid-I-Shar Mosque, built in the early seventeenth century and one of the most beautiful buildings of its kind in the world. It is entirely faced with tiles of the most brilliant colours and intricate patterns. We removed our boots at the entrance, then wandered along the beautiful colonnade which is tiled from floor to ceiling, with blue the predominating colour. The polished dome stands 176 feet above the ground and the entrance minarets are 160 feet high. By the time we had finished admiring them we were suffering from kinked necks.

We were taking photos of the beautiful mosaic inscriptions from the Koran on the interior of one of the domes when a tourist bus pulled up at the entrance and spilled its American tourists into the mosque. We four were mistaken for pilgrims as the camera-loaded tourists swarmed past to see the mosque. I nudged the boys,

"Aren't you going to speak to your countrymen?"

"Not likely. Look at them! Seven day globe-trotters. They wouldn't have time to stop and talk."

We entertained ourselves by following the tourist group about the mosque and watching them hurriedly photographing and discussing the architecture. On leaving the mosque, we met the two bearded and weather beaten Germans who were travelling in the Fiat. They had reached Isfahan but their troubles were not over yet – the mechanic had to repair the machine sufficiently to get them into Europe over many miles of rough country.

In the centre of the city is the Shar Square – once a great polo ground, but now a place of fountains, parks and gardens and almost ringed with mosques. We spent the rest of the morning visiting the biggest and best of them, including the Lutfullah Mosque and the Juma Mosque, the oldest building in the city.

*****

We had an enjoyable four days in the ancient capital then said goodbye to our American and German friends and headed north. Not far out of Isfahan the bitumen ended, like a dream, and we came to grips with the dust and corrugations once again. The country generally, was greener and the rain had brought the wild flowers out in profusion, the valleys were carpeted with red and yellow poppies. Nearing Qom the road became a nightmare, as dozens of buses passed and showered stones and dirt over us.

It was late evening when we sighted Qom and rode into the jammed streets. There seemed to be a big festival in progress, judging by the swarms of people. There were people from all parts of the Middle East including Arabs and Bedouin tribesmen with their long, white, flowing robes. In the centre of the city a big blue mosque with a gold spire stood out above everything else and in the reddening sunset looked most spectacular.

We decided to buy some food for dinner and then ride outside the city, camp and return next morning to have a look at Qom in the daylight. Looking for a parking place in the crowded street, I felt a little uncomfortable as some of the crowd jeered at us as we passed.

I found a spot in the city square beside a number of cars and had barely stopped when a mob closed in on us. They looked in a particularly nasty mood and stood around us shouting and shaking their fists at us before trying to upend our scooter.

We were unable to move, so we just stood there, straddling Mirra. The situation was at breaking point, when a dozen policeman, armed with long wooden truncheons charged into the mob, dispersing them with savage blows.

The police threw a cordon around us and the sergeant came forward and asked us in broken English what we wanted.

"Food, we said, "that is all."

He understood, then appointed an escort to take us to the market place while the remaining police guarded the scooter.

The market place was packed to overflowing and the police pushed ahead, clearing a way for us. We bought chappatis, salt, fish and some onions and then returned to our scooter under escort. I would dearly have liked to photograph some of the colourful characters we saw, but to produce a camera in front of them would have been asking for trouble.

When a corridor had been cleared for us, I twisted the throttle and rode off through the wildly gesticulating crowd. We still had not found out what all the fuss was about but we would probably have a chance tomorrow morning as we had to come back to the outskirts to refuel.

We packed early next morning and drove cautiously back to a garage. The attendant who greeted us, eyed us suspiciously for a moment, then brought the manager who spoke English.

"Come into my office and have tea with me and tell me what you are doing in Qom at a time like this."

"Tell us what is going on in town. We were mobbed last night."

"You mean you didn't know? One of the religious leaders of the country has just died and the city is in a week of mourning, as Qom is the religious capital of Persia."

"Oh!" we said, "that explains all those packed buses that passed us heading towards Qom and the great variety of people in the city."

"We had ideas of taking a look at the town but I guess we had better forget it," I said.

The manager looked thoughtful for a moment then said,

"It would be interesting for you to see what is going on in Qom. I tell you what we will do, if you promise to obey."

"Yes!" we said.

"I will let you go into Qom in one of my trucks with one of my trusted drivers if you promise not to leave the truck, or wind down the windows, and to do what he says." Keith and I glanced at each other, then nodded our heads.

A short, solid-looking Persian built like a wrestler entered, and after introductions we climbed into a big petrol wagon and were on our way.

First we were driven round the outskirts of Qom where we were able to view the city and the great mosque from a distance. The driver had a go at getting the big truck past the mosque but the road was blocked off by thousands of people, so we detoured and drove towards the square. At the square entrance, we were again brought to a standstill by the surging crowd.

Just then a mourners' procession started to move out of the mosque and along the main street towards the square. The line was four and five abreast and all the men were dressed in black, even to their skullcaps. Mourners carrying banners depicting birds, animals and dragons were scattered along the line. The procession moved along slowly, advancing only a few yards at a time. After stopping and chanting, professional mourners moved along the line spurring on the others and working them into a frenzy. By the time the line was halfway past us they had worked themselves up to such a pitch that they were tearing their clothes off. As they chanted they beat their chests with such ferocity that the skin was red raw and the thumping noise sounded like dozens of drums.

This had the expected affect on the crowd and they too were joining in the chanting and the procession. Several times some of the crowd showed an unfriendly interest in us and our driver, but we ignored them. Our driver was now becoming uneasy and said that he hoped they would not try and up-end the truck.

It took almost an hour for the procession to pass and we were only able to move very slowly, with the horn blowing all the way.

We eventually broke clear and gave a sigh of relief when we

reached the garage. The manager had been right, it was quite an experience, and we felt lucky to be in one piece. Before allowing us to leave, the manager gave us a sample of Persian hospitality by filling our petrol tanks and buying us two large loaves of bread, the first we had seen since Karachi. We told him one would be sufficient but he insisted and we had to try and squeeze the two into our already full rucksacks.

Halfway to Tehran we had petrol trouble, dirt in the filter bowl. After we fixed this we proceeded another five miles before getting a puncture. The gear was unloaded, the puncture fixed, the gear reloaded, and we were off again. A few miles further on, another puncture, this time in the front wheel. It looked as though this was not our day. It was blistering hot and the air was thick with flies. With the aid of some helpful soldiers from a nearby army post, the puncture was mended and we were again on our way.

We were dogged by tyre troubles for the rest of the day however, and we had to settle for a bed in the sand hills, within sight of the twinkling lights of Tehran.

The traffic of Isfahan seemed lawless, but it had nothing on Tehran, for the place was crammed with cars which hurtled along both narrow and wide streets, breaking every known road law. Mirrabooka was not the fastest off the mark now, and several times we were almost run down by careering trucks and cars while attempting to cross intersections.

By pure luck, we found our way to the British Embassy, and after filling in some forms set off to find a hotel that had been recommended to us. It was halfway along a narrow one-way street, with an oily little multi-lingual Persian as Manager.

"I can give you a room on the top floor which overlooks the street," he said.

We followed him up the spiral staircase and along a dimly lit hall at the end of which was a room with a large bay window and reasonable furniture. We had our passports taken for police inspection and were given the usual forms to fill in.

Keith stayed to organise the room while I went to find a garage for Mirrabooka. I was told there was one down the street at the end of a lane-way, but I found it impossible to get near it as the way was completely blocked by traffic. I checked to see if there was another way into the place and a helpful youth offered to guide me there.

It was good of him, I thought, but I changed my mind when he directed me right into the flow of oncoming traffic in a one-way street. The only thing I could do was to carry on to the first turnoff, for to turn around in the tide, would have meant a sticky end. The moments I spent in that street were some of the most anxious of the whole trip. We eventually found the garage and after a talk with the proprietor left Mirrabooka in his care and returned to the hotel.

It was now lunchtime and we were lucky to find a café open, for between 1.00 and 4.00 p.m. everything stops for a siesta to prepare for the nightlife.

We ate a steak lunch, then took a stroll around the sleeping city. Walking along one of the quiet avenues we came to a building with a tourist sign outside.

"What do you reckon, will we try for a map?" I said.

"Yes, and see what else they have to offer," said Keith.

The office on the first floor was large and well equipped. A sharp, polished, well-dressed Teherani with a toothbrush moustache stood behind the desk.

"Yes Sirs. Can I help you?" he said, displaying a beautiful set of dentures.

We told him what we wanted.

"Here you are Sirs, maps and tourist guide to Tehran. Could I interest you in a special tour of Tehran's inaccessible spots? We have the city sights, palace, wrestling stadium, museum, mosques and the nearby mountain resorts – or a tour of the night clubs of Tehran?"

Keith and I looked at each other.

"How much?" I said, trying to look as suspicious as I could. He rattled off a list of prices, telling us again what we could get for our money.

"No thanks, you can keep it. Come on Keith."

Before we reached the top of the stairs, the price had dropped to a quarter of the original.

"Tell you what I will do," he said, "I will take you on all the tours, and show you the night clubs at no extra cost. What do you say?"

"And the price?"

"The same," he said.

We took his offer feeling we were sticking our necks out, but if he took us to all the places he said he would, at the price, we would be well in front – but we would have to be careful.

At 1.00 p.m. sharp the following afternoon Mr. 'Tourist-Catcher' picked us up in a taxi and off we went. After a quick run round the new and old parts of the city we were taken to the palace in time to see the changing of the guard. Making the most of the opportunity I attempted to take a photo, but was almost arrested by a policeman, as I did not have a permit. This made 'Catch'em' very unhappy as we drove off around the palace grounds to the old palace. We were stopped at the big gates and checked by a guard. Catch'em tipped the guard and he allowed us to pass. The taxi parked in the enormous square courtyard which has four hundred doors opening into it. Behind these doors, so we were told, previous Shahs once kept their harem, but today the rooms are empty. Catch'em tipped another two guards and we were allowed to enter the main banquet hall which is now a museum and amongst the richest rooms in the world.

The great hall was packed with treasures acquired legitimately, and otherwise, by past rulers. Around the high walls hung irreplaceable tapestries and paintings, while the furniture ranged from solid gold tables to chairs of teak and ivory. At the far end of the hall on a raised platform stood the fabulous Peacock Throne. In order to get a closer look it was necessary to tip one of the guards who had been following us closely. It seemed unbelievable that we were standing before the throne that had been carried off by the Persian Invader Nadir Shar in 1739 from the Fort at Delhi. Using Catch'em as an interpreter, we found out that the throne had taken seven years to build and although the Persian would not admit it, the throne was a perfect example of Mogul art. The Peacock Throne gets its name from the figures of two peacocks standing behind it with their tails outspread. The figures are inlaid with sapphires, rubies, emeralds, pearls and other precious stones representing the natural colours of the birds. Seeing the throne and the palace alone had justified our decision to step out with Catch'em. I tried to sneak a photo but was caught in the act and had to tip the guard double the usual amount before I could press the shutter. We were shown around some of the other rooms with marble pillars and beautifully inlaid marble floors, then returned to the waiting taxi.

Our next destination was the foothills of the Elburz Mountains and the playground of Tehran. The road climbed up through forests for another two thousand feet and the air became cold and crisp. Fast flowing streams and waterfalls tumbled down the mountainside and perched on the mountainsides were millionaire chalets.

The taxi pulled into the grounds of 'The' hotel and we were allowed to get out and have a look around. A hundred feet above us was a large snowfield where guests were enjoying themselves in the snow. I broke away from the rest of the party and went for a quick walk through the hotel and was harassed by the doorman.

Returning to the city along the tree-lined avenues, we passed luxury homes, Embassies and visited several mosques before pulling up at the wrestling stadium.

Of all the stadiums in the world, this must be the most elaborate, for the interior is lined with mosaic tiles and cut glass. Wrestling is an ancient sport of the Persians and they have glorified it in building this mosque-like stadium. The main arena is only about fifteen to twenty feet wide but it is lavishly decorated with rugs and tapestries. Only the elite of Tehran visit the stadium and at one end of the stadium is the Shah's personal box. A splendid relief of a group of wrestlers decorates one wall.

We were invited to step into the gym to see the huge dumbbells which the wrestlers use to limber up before stepping into the ring. Some of them were four feet high and it was enough for us to try and lift one. At the far end of the gym two wrestlers were having a workout with similar dumbbells – but they were tossing them around their bodies as though they were made of balsa wood.

Catch'em arrived at our hotel at 8.00 p.m. to take us on our tour of the city's night clubs, "at no extra charge." Walking down the busy street he explained to us that there were three classes of nightclubs in Tehran and suggested we start at the bottom and work our way up. Keith and I looked at each other.

"Lead on."

"Feeling hungry?" Catch'em asked and suggested we find a café.

The café he selected was a large underground one with a ceiling of huge wooden bearers. The customers consisted mostly of men, and were a most unhappy bunch.

We sat down at a table and a waiter in a greasy uniform came to take our order. Keith and I were not very hungry and only ordered some Shish-kebab. Catch'em seemed disappointed at our order and apologised for taking us into such a poor restaurant and suggested we go to another place before the food arrived.

Walking along the maze of narrow busy streets, we passed many of the famed nightclubs where weird wailing Persian music drifted up from out of the cellars along with various aromas.

Catch'em stopped in front of a heavily decorated doorway and beckoned us to follow him.

"Looks like this is it!" I said and we squeezed past the bouncers blocking the narrow entrance, then followed on down the spiral staircase into the nightclub below.

The place was packed and we had to literally cut our way through the smoky atmosphere. The room was a long thin one and we found ourselves a table by the far wall and settled down. The company could be described as uncertain.

Sitting at the table opposite was a group of sailors who were being entertained by a buxom Persian girl, and there were even a few Turks and Arabs. In front of us was the stage on which was a five-piece band playing an odd collection of instruments and accompanying a sultry Turkish girl who was wailing in tune to the music in a deep contralto voice. Long black hair fell over her face as she wriggled her way across the stage and brought cries of delight from her male audience. A waiter came to take our drink orders and Catch'em suggested we sample a purple brew which some of the inebriates were drinking. We settled for Pepsi Cola, much to his disgust. Whatever they were drinking was certainly taking its toll, for many of the customers were prostrate across the tables.

Our presence was eventually noted by some of the customers who gradually crept forward on us muttering softly. When the Turkish girl had finished her number, another artiste came on. She was a woman of about thirteen stone with hair dyed yellow. The tall, longhaired bandleader opened with a few squeaky chords from his clarinet and the rest of the band joined in with the singer. The bandleader looked the part with his big, black bushy eyebrows and his gold and silver teeth which he took great pleasure in flashing.

Halfway through the number the weighty vocalist spotted Keith and proceeded to give him the glad eye for the rest of her number, hardly taking her eyes off him as she wriggled in time with the music. I nudged Keith,

"Hey, you have won yourself a heart," I whispered.

"Not bloody likely," was the reply.

The bandleader saw what was going on and started raising his bushy eyebrows at Keith and flashing his teeth. The heavyweight vocalist had hardly sung the last note when she bounced off the stage and made straight for Keith and proceeded to stroke his red beard.

Keith resisted with a stern face and sat unmoved. Catch'em thought it a great joke and was cackling like a broody hen. However, my mind was snapped away from all this when I felt a hand on my hip pocket. I turned around to see a lean looking character trying to lift my red notebook, which he mistook for a wallet. I swung my chair around and put the back of it in front of me and leant back onto the wall.

The situation reached its climax with the singer sitting in Keith's lap and my being surrounded with pickpockets. Keith was trying to get rid of his admirer by bouncing her off, but she was pretty hefty.

"Better call them off and let's get out of here and find some place else," I said, thinking that this may be the only way we could reach the street in one piece.

"What, don't you like?" he said in a hurt tone.

"No we don't like," Keith echoed.

Catch'em spoke to the girl and she backed off and stood

beside the pickpockets. We paid up and started to leave, but on the way to the door Keith was harassed by the singer while I had my own escort. Somehow we managed to reach the street where Catch'em apologised for taking us into such a terrible place.

"No more," we said, but he followed us up the street begging us to allow him to show us one of the better class nightclubs so that we would not go away with a bad impression of the city.

To get rid of him, we agreed. The nightclub was very near first class but when Catch'em saw that we were not going to pay for his entertainment he quickly lost interest in us and suggested we finish the tour and stormed off. It was after midnight when we reached our hotel and in spite of everything, we felt the evening had been a worthwhile experience.

I had my first upset for the new day when I went to collect our passports from the manager.

"I have not got them. The police have."

"Rubbish. I want them now. You have had them for five days, besides we are leaving now."

The once pleasant little man now turned very surly.

"It would be better for you if you stayed on."

"Very well, I will have to go to the police and see about them," I said.

"Wait," he said, staring savagely at me. "I have them here," then slapped them on the counter.

I felt like saying a lot, but that would not have helped so I quickly grabbed them and checked to see that they were in order.

The loading up operation almost caused a major traffic jam as a great crowd gathered round, some of their number offering to help us. The confusion attracted the police who moved in to see what was causing the hold-up. It was some time before we were able to get away, as the police made us account for our movements from the time we had left Pakistan.

We had hoped to visit the Caspian Sea, but this was out of bounds to us because it was a military area.

Ninety miles from Tehran the bitumen ended and we crossed miles of road which had been sealed with oil from the nearby wells. The soil became a deep rich brown in colour and, watered by snow fed streams from the Elburz, it supported fine crops of wheat and grapes.

By evening the clumps of trees became more frequent and when we saw trees accompanied by soft grass and a fast flowing stream nearby, we made camp. It was the best campsite we had had for months. There was wood and water in abundance. "Let's have a good cook-up," Keith said, grabbing the water bucket and making for the stream. I armed myself with a machete and went to fetch the wood.

About a hundred yards away from the camp on the banks of the stream, I found a big pile of driftwood, just what I wanted. I stuck the machete in the ground and started to drag some of the heavier timber free. I had just reefed a big branch away when I almost froze to the spot, for no more than five feet away from me, lying coiled up amongst the timber was a great two-toned grey snake. It instantly unravelled itself and struck a menacing pose with an arched neck and head waving to and fro, waiting its chance to make a strike. At the same instant as this happened, I whipped off my crash helmet and, holding it by the inside webbing, held it in front of me so that if it struck it would have to bite on the fibreglass first.

I was not sure what type of snake it was but I was not going to take any chances as it looked very big and healthy. It made several feints at me as I edged back towards the machete which was about six feet away – all the time keeping my eyes on the swaying reptile. Reaching for the knife, I flicked my eyes towards it and the snake struck. It fell just short of my crash helmet as I had moved a little out of range. Sensing that I was armed, it turned and made for the water. For the first time I could see all of it – a good seven feet and very thick. When I had recovered, I cautiously finished gathering the wood.

Crossing the desert – South Persia (inspecting the air spring)

'The roofs of the adobe domes ... and from the distance, looked like giant anthills ...'

'In its day, the fort must have been an invincible stronghold ... '

The Eyes of the Stupa of Bodh-nath

Town Square in Kerman, Southern Persia (Statue of Shah in background)

Keith was waiting for me with a box of matches in his hand.

"What kept you?"

"I disturbed a snake and had to go a few rounds."

"Very big?" Keith asked.

"Big enough," I answered. Our spot was too good to be chased off by a snake.

While we were cooking our stew, we had more visitors – a family of three mongooses. They scurried around the camp, playing tag with each other, taking little or no notice of us. We now felt a little easier about the snake, for with these three terrors around no respectable snake would dare visit us – we hoped.

The next morning was fine and very cold as we set out over the rough and badly-corrugated road to Tabriz, where we stopped long enough to replenish supplies.

The track across the salt pans was scorching hot under the midday sun and the glare terrific. The only signs of activity were camel trains marching for Khoi and an occasional deer or fox which would dart across our path.

Khoi is the village where visitors have to get their clearance from the police before proceeding to the Persian-Turkish frontier and the customs. Riding into the sleepy village we were stopped by a soldier armed with a submachine gun. He indicated that we were to go with him so we followed. We were led up a narrow lane, then he stood guard over the scooter while we went to have our interview in a building. When the formalities were completed, we were handed over to the sergeant who spoke six languages, including English. He looked more like a confidence man than a soldier, with his trim little moustache and bright blue and gold uniform. Grinning politely at us he said,

"I will want two more passport photos from you before you can go."

"What!" I said. "The police already have six photos of us now, besides we have no more."

We argued the point for half an hour but when we refused to go back to Tehran to get more photos taken, he said he would make an exception and allow us through.

"Do you want any petrol?" he asked. "If you do, you had better fill up here, there is no more until over the border."

Thinking we had seen the last of him we rode to the garage but on arrival we were startled to see him standing there – waiting for us.

"What are you doing here?"

"Me, I am the proprietor. How much fuel would you like?"

"Two gallons," I said, wondering how much we were going to be charged. I did not have to wonder long, ten shillings was the price. I could see it would be no good objecting so I quietly paid up.

"You will have to change your money into Turkish lire in Khoi," the sergeant said.

"No thanks. We will change our money on the border."

"Very well, but first you have to get a clearance from me, before you can leave Khoi and it would be better for you if you did change your money here."

We understood what he meant so we decided to humour him by letting him change our small coins, for we knew if he got hold of our other money that would be the end of it.

We dug into our pockets and showed him a bare handful of coins. Scoffing he said, "Where is the rest?"

"That is all we have," I said, hoping he would not search us.

We argued about the rate of exchange for some time but as the stakes were not high he gave in.

"Come, let us have coffee before you go, we are still good friends – yes?"

Entering the coffee-house, the sergeant ordered the customers out and we were left with the place to ourselves. We drank our coffee quietly, then nodding to Keith, I suggested we get moving. We got as far as the door when the sergeant stopped us.

"Wait. You have not paid for the coffee."

This was what he had been waiting for, to try and trap us into showing our concealed money.

"You invited us to drink with you, so you pay" said Keith.

"No, you pay or I arrest you."

At first I felt like calling his bluff but I looked outside and saw his armed men standing there.

"How much?" Keith asked the waiter.

Suddenly I remembered I still had some coins left in the petrol fund.

It was just enough. I handed it to the waiter then quickly made an exit. We were out of Khoi before the sergeant had time to speak again.

The Blue Mosque, Isfahan

The Blue Mosque, Isfahan, Persia

Inside the Blue Mosque, Isfahan

The Peacock Throne, Tehran, Persia

CHAPTER TEN

The joint Persian-Turkish Customs were set in a saddle between two high mountains, one on each side of the border, and each post sported a flag and lookout tower. The sun was at its zenith and blazed down on the enclosed courtyard, leaving us little shade in which to park Mirrabooka.

I had just switched the motor off when an officer came and told us it was siesta time and there would be no more clearances for three hours. That was it, so we confiscated the only shady spot beside a flight of cement steps and dozed off.

I woke up in about half an hour and, feeling very much awake, settled back to watch the Turkish and Persian guards who looked as though they were competing for a coveted trophy. By Persian standards, the Turk was smartly dressed and sweated heavily as he marched up and down the fence, with rifle on the shoulder, while the slovenly dressed Persian in oversized, baggy trousers and tunic, dragged his rifle along behind him. His boots were coming apart with the uppers barely holding onto the soles, and an 'about face' was almost fatal for them.

I got bored with the inactivity and took a stroll round the courtyard, leaving Keith to carry on with his nap. When I came to the fence, I made myself comfortable, leaning on it and proceeded to gaze across into Turkey.

I had been there for about ten minutes when I suddenly felt something sharp poking me in the ribs. I turned to see the Persian prodding me with his bayonet and waving me off the fence. He was not satisfied with this and stood guard over me for the rest of the time. Whenever I stood up he poked the bayonet under my nose and made me sit down again. I was glad when siesta time was over and I was able to part with his company.

Not far over the border we got our first view of Mount Ararat, the giant cone which rises to almost 17,000 feet. A violent storm was building up around it and lightning filled the sky, changing it to a murky green to the accompaniment of thunder claps which seemed to make the very air around us vibrate. As we rode, the mountain became more spectacular as the sky around it changed from green to inky black, standing out against the shining white cone.

Suddenly, we found ourselves engulfed in a hurricane that literally lifted us off the ground. I pulled up smartly. There was no shelter to be had anywhere so we cowered behind Mirrabooka. The wind stopped as quickly as it had started and then, without warning, we were in the grip of a hailstorm. Great chunks of ice pelted down on us and plinked and plonked on our crash helmets, bruising our shoulders.

"It couldn't happen to anybody but us," Keith screamed above the din. When the storm eventually abated we joked about the incident as we dried off.

It was dark when we rode into Dogubavazit and parked in front of a noisy restaurant. Entering the slush-lamp lit place, we squeezed through the crowd and took a seat beside two hungry looking Turks who were tearing chunks off a round flat loaf of bread, and stuffing it into their mouths. The waiter knew no English so I dug out my phrase book and tried ordering in Turkish. The only word I got right was 'Ekmek' – bread, and this was brought along with two cups of very thick black coffee. We found the bread very filling and by the time we had finished felt as though we had had a three-course meal. Finding out the price of the meal was almost impossible but fortunately there was an English-speaking army Officer close by who came to our rescue.

We rode into the night for about ten miles before we found a place to camp. It was bitterly cold and we lost no time in getting the tent up and diving into our sleeping bags.

We were woken at daybreak by two shepherds who poked their heads into the tent to see what it contained. Keith got a fright and became very annoyed and flourished the machete in front of their noses. They disappeared as quickly as they had come but crept back later on to watch us eat breakfast.

It was a beautiful day and the scenery was absolutely superb. The road crept upwards across alpine passes that were still slushy from the melting snow. One pass still had up to ten feet of snow piled up beside the road. On the lower slopes, green grass and red and yellow flowers were breaking through. In the valleys we passed isolated villages and small herds of cattle, something we had not seen for a long time.

Erzurum is another Turkish town that was over run by the conquerors of Asia Minor including the Romans, Greeks and Arabs. We reached Kara in the evening and pulled up at an open café opposite an army post. After brushing the dust off ourselves, we sat down at a table. All was quiet for five minutes then a tall, middle-aged man dressed in sports clothes approached us.

"From where are you coming?" he asked.

When we told him he looked puzzled for a moment then said,

"I am an officer from the Fort. Would you join us? We are about to eat."

We were given mutton and bread to eat while answering questions.

"What supplies do you take with you?" the officer asked.

Keith casually listed a number of items including methylated spirits for our stove and before he had time to finish, we were hustled off to the nearby grocers shop. The place was shut but it did not remain that way for long; the officer called and hammered on the door until the worried owner opened it. The grocer was swept back into his shop by a wave of the officer's men.

"Please, what is it you require for your journey," the officer said.

"Well ———" said Keith.

"Never mind," cut in the officer, "I will fix."

With the aid of his N.C.O.'s he stormed the shelves and selected what he considered would be best for us to carry. The grocer protested loudly, but it had no effect. It was almost impossible to stand in the tiny shop, for more and more curious spectators squeezed their way in to watch the show. Shelves began to collapse and everything from salami to dates rained down upon us. When eventually the shop was cleared, the place was a shambles with the poor grocer standing in the centre of it all, badly shaken and shocked by the sudden invasion.

While loading Mirrabooka, the fort's brass band struck up in the parade ground opposite,

"What do you think of our band?" the officer said.

"Wonderful," I said, ignoring the harsh discords. "The best band I've ever heard."

With near bursting eardrums, we thanked the officer and his men for their help and rode out of town.

Next morning we got away to an early start and set out for Gumusane and the long climb up over the 8,000 feet pass by Mount Kopdagi. It was hard to keep my eyes on the road and not the alpine scenery. This road is closed for eight months of the year and even though now it was mid spring, the snow was still piled up to twelve feet thick by the side of the road, making a white gorge for us to drive through. A snowplough had just cleared the track and the road was a quagmire.

The descent to Gumusane was breathtaking, particularly when our brake drums ran hot and I found the scooter coasting down the steep winding gravel road at forty miles per hour with no hope of stopping. How we reached the bottom intact, I will never know. When I eventually stopped, it would have been possible to grill a steak on the brake drums. We had been over a lot of grades, but this was by far the steepest. At the time I do not think Keith knew what was happening for he told me afterwards that he thought I had gone crazy, trying to take Mirrabooka down such a grade at that speed. We still had a lot of mountain ranges to cross and I was now feeling very wary about long, downhill grades.

At Gumusane, Keith decided to cash a cheque, so I parked in

front of the most prosperous looking bank and we entered. Cashing the cheque almost turned into a national crisis for no-one in the bank had ever seen a Traveller's cheque and they thought we were trying to put one over them. The police were called and we had our passports checked and we were cross-examined. To make matters worse, no-one had heard of Australia, and it was not until one of the elders of the town was brought that we were able to clear ourselves. The wise man of the village must have been very worldly for he had both heard of Australia and had seen Travellers Cheques. Keith got his money and we left, still being eyed suspiciously by the policeman.

From Gumusane the road continued to drop, passing through gorge after gorge, all of them sheer and colourful and with roaring rivers racing their way seaward and filling the gorge with the noise of their turbulent waters.

The road climbed to the Zigana Pass (6,600 feet) and skirted dozens of deep gorges and hairpin bends. Heavy black clouds lay ahead and the rumble of thunder indicated that there was a storm brewing. As we climbed, the views became more awe inspiring and the storm came closer. The mountainsides were clothed in pine forest and stood out against the white, driven snow of the high peaks. Mirrabooka chugged away merrily on the long grind and also seemed to be enjoying the change in altitude. Then the storm broke over us and we were again buffeted by wind gusts that almost stopped Mirrabooka in her tracks; one actually did. The storm stayed with us until we reached the Pass, filling the gorge with its eerie colours and booming echoes.

We pulled in beside a chalet, which had a sign out front, "Otel', and was set in a saddle between high, snow-capped peaks. A cold, biting wind was howling through the pass and we lost no time in garaging Mirrabooka and seeking refuge in the "Otel'.

The "Otel' was a two storied building of wood and stone with one large room and kitchen on the ground floor and sleeping quarters on the top floor. The big dining room was furnished with heavy tables and chairs and in the centre of the room was a cylindrical wood stove around which four soulful-looking men sat, drinking black coffee ... ...

*****

Early next morning we got fine views of the gorges to the south and northward to the Black Sea – before the cloud swirled back again, cutting us off from the outside world. We rugged up and started on the steep descent to the Black Sea, which was thirty-two miles away. The grade was almost as steep as the one from Askale. At about the three thousand feet mark, we broke out of the clouds and into brilliant sunshine, to discover we were running parallel with another deep gorge.

The road flattened out on the narrow coastal plain beside a swirling river.

Trabzon, known as the Green City of the Black Sea, is the old centre of the Sultans of the Ottoman Empire. To us, Trabzon seemed like a large lazy seaside town, typical of such resorts. The streets were narrow and cobble-stoned and in the centre of the town numerous restaurants opened onto the neat square with its park and fountains.

It was my turn to cash a cheque. I too had trouble, but was a little luckier. The bank manager spoke English.

Trabzon was interesting with its ancient mosques, castle and several early Christian churches which have now been converted into Mosques and Museums. Leaving the Green City we had trouble finding the way out and after making several attempts pulled up beside two men leaning against a post. In broken Turkish and sign language, we asked them which was the way to Samsun. We almost fell off the scooter when we got our reply.

"Round to the left then straight ahead, you can't miss it."

They were Americans from the rocket base.

The journey along the coast was unforgettable for two reasons – the scenery and the delinquents. The former was very wonderful, with the high mountains sweeping down to the water's edge and lining the foreshore with high cliffs and deep coves. The vegetation was thick and the road was crossed by many fast flowing streams.

The delinquents of the coast played a game which neither we nor anybody else travelling these roads thought funny. The game consisted of throwing rocks at passing cars, trucks, motor scooters, in fact anything that moved. Not only did they throw stones but they actually bombarded the passers-by with rocks that were many inches in diameter. Riding along, we would come to groups of these harmless looking boys standing by the roadside with their hands behind their backs gazing innocently around as we approached. As soon as we were past, we would be showered with rocks. In most cases there was very little we could do and we had to rely on their aim and the speed of Mirrabooka to get us out of trouble. On more than one occasion we were thankful for our crash helmets as large rocks crashed onto them.

We passed several cars on the road that looked as though they had been machine-gunned, and several had had windows smashed. We were told the only way we could get our own back was to catch the culprits, if that was possible, and take their trousers off and tear them in half. This apparently was the worst humiliation they could suffer. We got close several times but were never able to effect the full punishment, for once the boys knew we were after them, we had little hope of catching them.

At dusk we were able to find a grass-carpeted campsite by a small stream. We put the tent up and got a fire going, well out of sight of the road. We were drinking our last cup of tea by the firelight when we heard twigs crackling on either side of us and two faces appeared out of the dark. I quickly shone my torch on the figures, who turned out to be two youths who had apparently seen our glowing fire and had come to investigate. They were not very talkative and they disappeared as quickly as they had come.

We were woken at daybreak by the sound of voices and the munching of cows. We poked our heads out of the tent to see the two prowlers had returned with about twenty of their mates. We were also surrounded by a herd of cows and two of them had taken a fancy to Mirrabooka and were washing her with their tongues. We packed before having breakfast so as not to lose anything.

The narrow road followed the coast over the high, steep cliffs and whenever we came to a river a large detour upstream was necessary before making a crossing over a dilapidated bridge, most of which had planks missing. The road generally was very narrow and in most places there was barely enough room for two cars to pass.

It was along these narrow stretches where the stone throwing delinquents would lie in wait for us. On one occasion, we were entering a narrow cutting with high earth banks when I looked up in time to see a boy on the crest of the cutting with a huge sod of red dirt in his hands ready to drop it on us as we passed underneath. It seemed as though we had little hope of escape but his timing was a little out, and I opened the throttle and shocked Mirrabooka into life. The rear wheel spun on the loose gravel and showered grit as I dodged the plummeting sod, which missed us by inches. Keith shouted abuse from the pillion as the boy's mates appeared and commenced bombarding us with stones. Fortunately for us Mirrabooka outpaced most of them, although Keith was unlucky enough to stop a few in the back.

The land was cultivated right to the water's edge in places and it was strange to see crops growing right on the seashore. On the little beaches, fishermen were hauling in tuna or mending their boats and nets. On the other side of the road grew groves of hazel nuts.

The Black Sea cafés might be compared with western fish and chip shops, with the exception that they served shish-kebab, dolman, yoghurt and cay-tea. We liked eating in these places for at least we could see what we were getting and usually were invited to make our own selection.

From Ordu to Samsun the road flattened out and we got into the swamp country. Many times we felt we were back in India as we rode over the broken, waterlogged roads dodging stupid buffaloes. The living conditions had also deteriorated, and the people appeared to be not much better off than some of the Indian peasants. It was a relief to get out of the foul smelling swamp country and back onto higher ground.

Early one afternoon we reached Samsun, a city built on the side of a steep hill, and whose history dates back to the Bronze Age. Samsun had a fine harbour and well laid out parks and gardens along the foreshore, with a two feet six inch gauge railway running from the wharves to the interior. In one of the parks a statue of Ataturk stands on the spot where he sparked off the war for Turkish Independence in 1919.

There are the familiar mosques and narrow cobblestone streets, but modern buildings are creeping in amongst the old and in many places one could almost imagine that we were in a Western city ... ...

*****

The greasy Turkish food caught up with us shortly after leaving Samsun and for a few days we were suffering from sick stomachs.

After a hard, dusty ride, we reached the old copper town of

Corum, built on steep hillsides. It was most noticeable that the male population spent their time sitting in clay houses, drinking, while the women toiled in the fields, and did the work for the men, who seemed an uncomprehending lot.

Our way through central Turkey lay across open, undulating plains and pine forested hills that smelt clean and fresh after the dusty heat of the plains. Colourful birds flew amongst the forests while the plains were plagued with flies.

We arrived in Ankara at 4.00 p.m. one afternoon and began looking for accommodation. By coincidence we parked in front of a place which had the title of "Tourist Information Centre" and went to investigate. A receptionist who could speak English dragged out a long list of hotels and proceeded to run through the price list, starting from the top.

We picked one that seemed reasonable and were surprised to find that it was the building next door.

The receptionist made it easier for us by ringing the hotel to see if we could get a room, and then informed us that there was one available on the fifth floor for 7.50 lira or 5/6 a day. We said we would take it and went to see our room.

The hotel was quite modern and even had two elevators. Our room was large and comfortable, with an adjoining bathroom and a large balcony from which we had excellent views of the historic

Roman Baths in the allotment next door. Later on we were to sit on this balcony and watch tourists being taken on conducted tours of the baths. As the tours were all conducted in Turkish or German, we felt we were just as well off on our balcony.

The first thing was to get cleaned up, so we took turns in the bathroom to bath and wash our clothes.

"I bet the people on the third floor have trouble with silted pipes after this lot," Keith said as he left the bathroom with a bundle of washing.

We put on our city wear and set off on foot to explore Ankara. The city is very westernised with spacious streets, trolley buses, heavy traffic and traffic lights, for which we were most thankful. We felt a bit out of place for a while but it did not take too long to adjust ourselves to the bustling city life. We had dinner in a small café then returned to the neon-lit city and wandered along through the crowds of people who had come out to enjoy the cool of the evening. The wide footpaths were cluttered up with shoeshine boys and their elaborate equipment, which they polished in between customers and the business of getting customers. Fruit and peanut vendors were prevalent and we had to weave our way through their ranks in places to dodge them.

There seemed to be something on, for streams of people were heading in the direction of the brightly-lit end of the city, so we decided to follow. The attraction was the Youth Park which is built around an artificial lake and surrounded by a large parkland which was now festooned with colourful lights. We paid our admission fee and joined the thousands of visitors streaming into the grounds, and walked with them along the winding pathways. Hot dog and ice cream stands were scattered amongst the trees, and loud speakers filled the air with Turkish music. Open-air restaurants were spread around the lake and at the far end of the grounds was Side-Show Alley with all the usual attractions one expects to find in such a place. It was a big change from the previous evening, for now we got into the carnival mood and mixed with the crowds eating ice creams and hot dogs.

We used Mirrabooka when possible, to travel around the city. A visit to the hill on the outskirts where Ataturk's Mausoleum stands was a must. It was a huge place constructed of large, light coloured sandstone blocks with practically no ornamentation. We parked, and mixed with a large party of pilgrims who had just arrived and moved with them to the Mausoleum. However, we had not gone too far when we attracted the attention of two guards, who by the look of them thought we had come to sabotage the place.

Without speaking, they separated us from the main party and escorted us around the Mausoleum, not allowing us to touch anything. When we had completed the circuit we were made to return the way we had come even though we were only twenty yards from our scooter.

Ataturk's residence was close by so we joined the long queue of people reverently filing through the grounds and the old house. On entering, we were again placed under guard and very nearly had my camera confiscated, but after a silent battle managed to retain it.

"Suspicious lot, aren't they? Do we look that bad?" said Keith.

In spite of the company we enjoyed inspecting the old two storied home with its collection of antique furniture and picturesque surroundings.

Mirabooka was in need of some overdue attention and the thought of a "Rabbit" agent in Istanbul made us cut short our stay in Ankara. The electric starter button had disintegrated and now the machine was started by touching two loose wires, a thing that astounded the villagers. We had thrown two tyres and tubes away and now our existing rubber was not much better.

Our scooter agent went under the name of Basiret Genel Ticaret Ltd. and we found them on the second floor of an old building in a collection of musty offices. They were most interested in our machine and suggested we leave it with them while we settled in.

The hotel to which we were taken was very nice, in fact far too quiet compared to what we had been used to – so we went in search of something more suitable. The place we selected turned out to be a little more lively than we expected. It was a quaint four-storied hotel which overlooked a tiny square – and a bus terminus. After we had spent a few nights in our room, above the street, we began to wish we had not moved in. The din from the square lasted twenty-four hours a day as great crowds of people carrying bundles pushed their way onto waiting buses. The line of buses extended from the square along a side street, and for most of the time there were at least twenty of them queued up. On the second day, we found out where the buses were going. They were taking pilgrims to Qom.

Istanbul is accounted one of the most beautiful cities in the world and the meeting place of the East and West. It was founded in 657 B.C. and since then had been ruled by the Greeks and Romans, was sacked by the Crusaders in 1204 and later taken into the Ottoman Empire in 1453. Today it is a predominately Muslim city with over 500 mosques, as well as ancient Roman walls and fabulous palaces and castles built by reigning Sultans between the fifteenth and nineteenth centuries.

Visits to the huge Kapah Carsi, or covered market place, to purchase food were frequent, for here we were able to see all the exotic merchandise of the East, including rugs, gold and silver, jewels, and precious antiques.

The six tall minarets of the Mosque of Sultan Ahmet, or Blue Mosque, situated on a hill overlooking the Golden Horn, attracted us from our arrival in Istanbul and at the first opportunity we paid it a visit. The mosque is enormous and is covered with blue tiles. Although beautiful, I still felt the Masjid-I-Shah mosque in Isfahan was the finest we had seen.

"You must make a trip on the Bosphorus. A visit to Istanbul is not complete unless you do."

We were told this by numerous people so we set aside a day to make the voyage.

The Port of Istanbul is big and busy and it was some time before we located the Black Sea Ferry. As luck would have it, we had barely settled ourselves when the weather closed in and a steady drizzle began, cutting visibility down to the water front.

The ferries of the Bosphorus act as a train or bus service and travel the length of the Strait calling at landing stages, there being about twelve on either side of the Strait. Black coffee is served on the voyage and there is a friendly carefree atmosphere, one that usually goes with a service of this nature. Along the southern shores of the Bosphorus, palaces decorate the waterfront displaying their marbled terraces and stately towering walls. On the hills behind, great grey stone castles and fortresses dominate the skyline.

Nearing the Black Sea, the Ferry swung into a channel between mine fields and steamed toward the last station on the run, situated on the corner where the Bosphorus meets the Black Sea. There was only a handful of passengers left to disembark – half of them tourists. Before leaving we were told to stay within sight of the ferry and the two cafés which stood close by. The area seemed heavily guarded, for no matter which way we looked we could see armed naval men wandering amongst the trees.

We paid one of the cafés a visit and, as we still had two hours to fill in, went for a stroll around our restricted area. Along the water's edge picturesque fishing boats were moored, while in the trees close by their recently used nets were drying out. The light was just right and it looked a perfect calendar picture. I looked around – there was no one in sight so I opened the camera. I was about to press the shutter when a large pair of hands loomed up over the lens and grasped my camera. I looked up to see a marine standing over me, trying to wrest the camera from me. I hung on for dear life, trying to explain that I meant no harm and I wanted my camera.

He finally let go and I hugged my camera while he delivered a lecture in Turkish to me and waved a bayonet under my nose.

I was very nearly arrested, but after a counsel with an officer, I was placed under guard until the ferry departed.

The waters of the Bosphorus teem with fish; consequently there is an abundance of fish in the market place and on the wharf and boats where they are kept alive in barrels of water so that you may choose the fish you like as it swims.

It was our last night in Istanbul and we had again accidentally met up with Don, the American hitchhiker and the two Germans with the battered Fiat.

"What say we go buy ourselves a fish meal on one of the boats and have our farewell dinner to Asia," said Don.

We all agreed, and set off to find a fishing boat with a large barrel full of big ones. The boat we selected was moored a short distance from shore and had to be reached by walking down a series of narrow springy planks. Under a canvas awning towards the stern stood a big wooden barrel with dozens of fish inside, fighting for survival in the confined space.

Trying to choose what we wanted was nearly impossible, so we told the boatman to pick five and cook them.

Making ourselves comfortable on the deck, we settled back to watch the boatman catch them. Fifteen minutes later – and very-much wetter, the boatman filleted our fish and stoked the coke fire to heat the hotplate. Round loaves of black bread and salt were produced and as the foot long fillets were cooked and handed out, we helped ourselves to the bread and salt.

The fish was beautiful, and as we ate, we tossed the bones over our shoulders into the Bosphorus. The last rays of the sun were disappearing, throwing a mantle of deep blue across the scene. We licked our fingers and paid one lira each for the fish as the voice of the muezzin wafted on the breeze from the direction of a minaret, calling the faithful to prayer.

Sheep in Eastern Turkey, Mt Ararat in background

Travelling through Eastern Turkey

On the road, Eastern Turkey

Eastern Turkey

Trabzon, on The Black Sea, North-east Turkey

The Black Sea, Northern Turkey coast

The Black Sea at Samsun, Northern Turkish coast

A Bay off The Bosphorus at Istanbul

Hagia Sophia in Istanbul

Ferries on The Bosphorus, Istanbul

THE END

www.ingramcontent.com/pod-product-compliance
Lightning Source LLC
Chambersburg PA
CBHW060458090426
42735CB00011B/2023